1001 Questions on the Bible

LARRY PIATT

BAKER BOOK HOUSE
Grand Rapids, Michigan 49506

ISBN: 0-8010-7085-6

Fourth printing, January 1988

All Scripture quotations are from the King James Version

Printed in the United States of America

Sample: Who was the first man?

      A. Joseph   B. Ezekiel   C. Moses   D. Adam

1. Who created the heavens and the earth?
   A. Adam   B. God   C. Eve   D. Abel

2. What did God create on the first day?
   A. Trees   B. Animals   C. The moon   D. Light

3. What did God do on the seventh day?
   A. Made Eden   B. Rested   C. Made plants   D. Made man

4. From what material did God make Adam?
   A. Plants   B. Monkeys   C. Water   D. Dust

5. What did God take from Adam to make the woman?
   A. A lip   B. A rib   C. His brain   D. A muscle

6. Who was the first woman?
   A. Eden   B. Ruth   C. Eve   D. Elisabeth

7. Who called the woman "Eve"?
   A. The serpent   B. God   C. Adam   D. Eve

8. Why was she called Eve?
   A. She was the first woman   B. She liked the name
   C. Eve means wife   D. She was the "mother of all living"

9. Where did Adam and Eve live?
   A. Garden of Gethsemane   B. Mt. Sinai   C. Utopia
   D. Garden of Eden

10. Who tempted Eve?
    A. Adam   B. The serpent   C. God   D. Abel

11. What did Eve eat?
    A. Banana
    B. Fruit from the tree of the knowledge of good and evil
    C. Apple   D. Fruit from the tree of life

12. With what did God clothe Adam and Eve?
    A. A cloud   B. Skins   C. His hand   D. Fig leaves

13. What guarded Eden?
    A. Soldiers   B. Snakes   C. Seraphim   D. Cherubim

14. Who were Adam and Eve's sons?
    A. Jacob and Esau   B. Cain and Abel   C. James and John
    D. Aaron and Moses

15. Who killed Abel?
   A. Adam   B. Cain   C. Eve   D. God

16. Who said, "Am I my brother's keeper"?
   A. Cain   B. Abel   C. God   D. Adam

17. Who was Adam's third son?
   A. Seth   B. Enoch   C. Abraham   D. Shem

18. What happened to Enoch?
   A. He lived 450 years   B. He died, having no children
   C. Nothing   D. He did not die.

19. Who was the oldest man in the Bible?
   A. Adam   B. Methuselah   C. Jared   D. Noah

20. How old was Methuselah when he died?
   A. 550   B. 1,000   C. 721   D. 969

21. Who built the ark?
   A. Moses   B. Noah   C. God   D. Jacob

22. Who were Noah's sons?
   A. Cain, Abel, and Seth   B. Peter, James, and John
   C. Reuben, Manasseh, and Judah   D. Shem, Ham, and Japheth

23. How many people were in the ark?
   A. 4   B. 8   C. 2   D. 6

24. How many days and nights did it rain?
   A. 30   B. 20   C. 50   D. 40

25. On what mountain did the ark land?
   A. Mt. Sinai   B. Mt. Ararat   C. Mt. Moriah   D. Mt. Horeb

26. What bird did Noah first send out of the ark?
   A. Dove   B. Owl   C. Raven   D. Sparrow

27. What bird did Noah send out next?
   A. Crow   B. Cardinal   C. Dove   D. Raven

28. How many times did Noah send this bird?
   A. 2   B. 1   C. 4   D. 3

29. What sign did God give to show He wouldn't flood the earth again?
   A. A star   B. A solar flare   C. A cloud   D. A rainbow

30. God gave people different languages to stop what building?
   A. The pyramids   B. The ark.   C. Idols   D. The Tower of Babel

31. What relation was Abraham to Lot?
   A. Brother   B. Father   C. Son   D. Uncle

32. Who was Abraham's wife?
    A. Sharon   B. Sarah   C. Rachel   D. Ruth

33. Why did Abraham and Lot separate?
    A. There was not enough land for both of them
    B. They wanted to stop their shepherds from fighting
    C. Lot wanted to go back home
    D. Abraham was tired of looking after Lot

34. Who was Sarah's handmaid?
    A. Leah   B. Hagar   C. Hannah   D. Mary

35. Who was Abraham and Hagar's son?
    A. Esau   B. Isaac   C. Jacob   D. Ishmael

36. How many people did the angels take out of Sodom?
    A. 4   B. 0   C. 3   D. 5

37. Who turned into a pillar of salt?
    A. Lot's wife   B. Lot's daughter   C. Lot's son   D. Lot

38. Who was Abraham and Sarah's son?
    A. Ishmael   B. Isaac   C. Isaiah   D. Ichabod

39. What does his name mean?
    A. At last   B. Laughter   C. Small one   D. Child of our old age

40. How old was Abraham when Isaac was born?
    A. 35   B. 75   C. 90   D. 100

41. How old was Sarah when Isaac was born?
    A. 55   B. 90   C. 100   D. 65

42. Why did Sarah want Hagar and Ishmael cast out?
    A. It was too crowded   B. Hagar hated her
    C. Hagar was lazy   D. Ishmael mocked Isaac

43. Where did Abraham attempt to sacrifice Isaac?
    A. Mt. Sinai   B. Mt. Moriah   C. Mt. Nebo   D. Mt. Horeb

44. Who stopped Abraham from offering Isaac?
    A. Sarah   B. Isaac   C. Lot   D. An angel

45. What did Abraham sacrifice instead of Isaac?
    A. A servant   B. A ram   C. A bull   D. A camel

46. How old was Sarah when she died?
    A. 75   B. 175   C. 127   D. 83

47. Who was Isaac's wife?
    A. Sarah   B. Esther   C. Rebekah   D. Rachel

48. How old was Abraham when he died?
    A. 100   B. 75   C. 204   D. 175

49. What were the names of Isaac's sons?
    A. Peter and Andrew   B. Cain and Abel
    C. James and John   D. Jacob and Esau

50. Which son did Isaac like better?
    A. Jacob   B. Esau   C. Abraham   D. Lot

51. Which son did Rebekah like better?
    A. Abraham   B. Jacob   C. Joseph   D. Esau

52. Who deceived Isaac for a blessing?
    A. Esau   B. Jacob   C. Adam   D. Ezra

53. What did Jacob use for a pillow?
    A. A sheep   B. A blanket   C. A saddle   D. A stone

54. What did Jacob see in a dream?
    A. Sheep   B. A ladder   C. Clouds   D. Esau

55. Whom did Jacob want to marry?
    A. Rebekah   B. Rachel   C. Leah   D. Sarah

56. How many years did Jacob serve for Rachel?
    A. 7   B. 5   C. 9   D. 3

57. Who was Rachel's father?
    A. Laban   B. Lot   C. Noah   D. Isaac

58. Who was Laban's sister?
    A. Sarah   B. Rebekah   C. Rachel   D. Leah

59. Whom did Jacob marry first?
    A. Rachel   B. Rebekah   C. Eve   D. Leah

60. How many more years did Jacob serve for Rachel?
    A. 17   B. 14   C. 7   D. 20

61. With whom did Jacob wrestle?
    A. An angel   B. Esau   C. Rachel   D. Leah

62. What was Jacob's new name?
    A. Joshua   B. Joseph   C. David   D. Israel

63. How many children did Jacob have?
    A. 12 sons, 1 daughter   B. 6 sons, 6 daughters
    C. 1 son, 12 daughters   D. 12 sons

64. Who was Rebekah's nurse?
    A. Dinah   B. Clara   C. Deborah   D. Donna

65. What was Esau's other name?
    A. Edom   B. Ezra   C. Israel   D. Reuben

66. Which of his sons did Jacob like best?
    A. Reuben   B. Benjamin   C. Joseph   D. Asher

67. What did Jacob give to his favorite son?
    A. A crown   B. Gold   C. A bar of silver
    D. A coat of many colors

68. Who persuaded Jacob's sons not to kill Joseph?
    A. Joseph   B. Simeon   C. Reuben   D. Judah

69. To whom did Joseph's brothers sell him?
    A. Canaanites   B. Hittites   C. Hivites   D. Ishmaelites

70. How much money did the brothers get for selling Joseph?
    A. 10 drachmas   B. 30 pieces of silver
    C. 20 pieces of silver   D. 20 pieces of gold

71. What did the brothers do with Joseph's coat?
    A. Dipped it in goat's blood   B. Sold it
    C. Hid it   D. Burned it

72. What did the brothers tell Jacob about Joseph?
    A. Joseph had been killed   B. Joseph was lost
    C. They had found a coat   D. Nothing

73. To whom did the caravan sell Joseph?
    A. Potiphar   B. Pharoah   C. Cleopatra   D. Jacob

74. Why did Potiphar throw Joseph into prison?
    A. Joseph was a Hebrew
    B. Joseph had lied to Potiphar
    C. Joseph had stolen a silver cup
    D. Potiphar's wife said Joseph attacked her

75. In prison, whose dreams did Joseph interpret?
    A. The butler's and baker's   B. The jailer's
    C. The butler's and maid's   D. His own dreams

76. Whom did Pharoah hang?
    A. Joseph   B. Potiphar   C. The butler   D. The baker

77. What did Pharoah's dream include?
    A. Dogs and cats   B. Money   C. Cattle and corn   D. Corn and beans

78. Who told Pharoah about Joseph?
    A. Potiphar   B. The baker   C. The butler   D. The jailer

79. What did Pharoah's dreams mean?
    A. Pharoah would be prosperous   B. A flood was coming
    C. There would be plenty of food and then famine
    D. Joseph did not know

80. What was Joseph's advice?
    A. To eat, drink, and be merry   B. To move
    C. Do not panic   D. To store grain

81. Whom did Pharoah appoint to store the grain?
    A. The butler   B. Joseph   C. Himself   D. Potiphar

82. How old was Joseph when Pharoah chose him?
    A. 17   B. 25   C. 40   D. 30

83. How many years of plenty were there?
    A. 14   B. 7   C. 5   D. 10

84. How many years of famine were there?
    A. 14   B. 10   C. 5   D. 7

85. What were the names of Joseph's sons?
    A. Jacob and Esau   B. Manasseh and Ephraim
    C. Ithamar and Eleazar   D. James and John

86. Why did Jacob's sons go to Egypt?
    A. To see the pyramids   B. They were moving to Egypt
    C. To buy food   D. To find Joseph

87. Which of Jacob's sons did not go to Egypt?
    A. Reuben   B. Gad   C. Benjamin   D. Naphtali

88. What were the brothers accused of in Egypt?
    A. Stealing   B. Killing   C. Idolatry   D. Spying

89. Which brother was kept in prison?
    A. Reuben   B. Dan   C. Levi   D. Simeon

90. Who were the brothers to bring on their next visit?
    A. Jacob   B. Rachel   C. Rahab   D. Benjamin

91. Why did Jacob's sons go to Egypt the second time?
    A. To get their brother out of prison   B. To buy more food
    C. To find Joseph   D. To find their lost grain

92. Who went with the brothers on their second trip?
    A. A guide   B. Jacob   C. Rachel   D. Benjamin

93. What was put in Benjamin's sack?
    A. Stones   B. Joseph's cup   C. A key   D. A map

94. What did Joseph do to his brothers?
    A. Put them in jail   B. Whipped them
    C. Made them slaves   D. Told them he was Joseph

95. Where did Jacob and his sons settle?
    A. Israel   B. Goshen   C. Palestine   D. Syria

96. What did Egyptians think of shepherds?
    A. They liked them   B. They considered them guardians of the gods
    C. They hated them   D. They worshiped them

97. How old was Jacob when he died?
    a. 100   B. 134   C. 147   D. 153

98. Jacob placed his right hand of blessing on which of Joseph's sons?
    A. Manasseh   B. Gershom   C. Issachar   D. Ephraim

99. How old was Joseph when he died?
    A. 90   B. 105   C. 76   D. 110

100. What plans did Joseph make for his bones?
    A. He wanted them left alone
    B. He wanted them carried out of Egypt
    C. He wanted them put in the sea
    D. He wanted them buried in a pyramid

101. Why did the Egyptians make the Israelites slaves? They were afraid
    the Israelites would:
    A. Make them slaves   B. Join their enemies and fight them
    C. Outnumber them   D. Leave Egypt

102. What did Pharoah tell the midwives to do?
    A. Kill the Hebrew daughters   B. Kill the Hebrew sons
    C. Kill the Egyptian daughters   D. Kill the Egyptian sons

103. The midwives disobeyed. What did they tell Pharoah when he asked
    them about it?
    A. They feared the Hebrews
    B. The Hebrews would not let them in
    C. They had forgotten
    D. The Hebrew women gave birth before they could arrive

104. What command did Pharoah give to the Israelites?
    A. To leave Egypt   B. To throw their sons into the river
    C. To throw their daughters into the river
    D. To worship the sun god

105. From what tribe were Moses' parents?
    A. Judah   B. Levi   C. Benjamin   D. Dan

106. What were the names of Moses' parents?
   A. Amram and Jochebed   B. Adam and Eve
   C. Eliab and Nahor   D. Isaac and Rebekah

107. How long did Moses' mother hide him after he was born?
   A. 3 months   B. 5 months   C. 7 months   D. 1 year

108. What did Moses' mother do when she could no longer hide him?
   A. Sent him to Pharoah   B. Left him with relatives
   C. Left him in the sand   D. Put him in an ark in the river

109. Who followed the baby?
   A. His mother   B. His sister   C. His brother   D. His father

110. Who was Moses' sister?
   A. Martha   B. Miriam   C. Marian   D. Mary

111. Who found the ark and the baby?
   A. Miriam   B. Pharoah's daughter   C. Aaron   D. Amram

112. Whom did Miriam get as a nurse for Moses?
   A. Aaron   B. Moses' mother   C. Pharoah's daughter   D. Herself

113. Why did Pharoah's daughter call the baby "Moses"?
   A. She had found him in an ark
   B. That was her grandfather's name
   C. Moses means "small one"
   D. She drew him from the water

114. What did Moses do when he saw an Egyptian beating a Hebrew?
   A. He hid   B. He killed the Egyptian
   C. He killed the Hebrew   D. He killed them both

115. Who did Moses see fighting the next day?
   A. Two Egyptians   B. Two Hebrews
   C. An Egyptian and a Hebrew   D. Two women

116. One of the men said something that upset Moses. What did he say?
   A. Do you intend to kill me, as you killed the Egyptian?
   B. Mind your own business   C. Pharoah wants to kill you
   D. Leave us alone

117. Where did Moses go after he fled from Egypt?
   A. Midian   B. Assyria   C. Israel   D. Palestine

118. Who was Moses' wife?
   A. Gad   B. Esther   C. Zappa   D. Zipporah

119. Who was her father?
   A. Joseph   B. Reuel   C. Ramses   D. Justin

120. Who was Moses' son?

    A. Levi   B. Gershom   C. Naphtali   D. Nun

121. What was Reuel's other name?

    A. Rabah   B. Jethro   C. Josiah   D. Jonah

122. As Moses was tending sheep, what sight caught his attention?

    A. A wounded lamb   B. A burning bush
    C. The sunset   D. A pillar of fire

123. On what mount did Moses see this sight?

    A. Mt. Olivet   B. Mt. Ararat   C. Mt. Nebo   D. Mt. Horeb

124. What did the Lord tell Moses to do?

    A. To write the Ten Commandments
    B. To go to Egypt and deliver Israel.
    C. To contact Miriam   D. To make an altar

125. God described the land that the Israelites would be going to as "a land flowing" with _____.

    A. Heavenly nectar   B. Milk and honey
    C. Wealth untold   D. Beautiful lilies

126. Whom did God appoint as Moses' spokesman?

    A. God   B. Miriam   C. Joshua   D. Aaron

127. Who told Aaron to meet Moses in the wilderness?

    A. Moses   B. A messenger   C. Miriam   D. God

128. When Moses and Aaron asked Pharoah to let the Israelites go into the wilderness and sacrifice, what did Pharoah say?

    A. Return within seven days   B. Stay here and sacrifice
    C. Leave and never return
    D. I know not the Lord, neither will I let Israel go

129. How old was Moses when he asked Pharoah to let the Israelites go?

    A. 75   B. 66   C. 33   D. 80

130. Aaron threw down the rod and it became a snake. What happened to the magicians' rods?

    A. Nothing   B. They began to shake
    C. They became snakes   D. They became frogs

131. Then what happened to the magicians' rods?

    A. They stood up   B. They wriggled away
    C. Aaron's rod swallowed them   D. Nothing

132. What was the first plague?

    A. Murrain of beasts   B. Water to blood   C. Frogs   D. Locusts

133. What was the second plague?
    A. Lice   B. Murrain of beasts   C. Locusts   D. Frogs

134. What was the third plague?
    A. Frogs   B. Lice   C. Flies   D. Darkness

135. What was the fourth plague?
    A. Frogs   B. Flies   C. Lice   D. Darkness

136. Which plagues did the magicians duplicate?
    A. Hail and darkness   B. Water to blood and frogs
    C. Water to blood and flies   D. Boils and locusts

137. Which was the first plague in which the Israelites' land, Goshen, was not affected?
    A. Frogs   B. Lice   C. Locusts   D. Flies

138. What was the fifth plague?
    A. Darkness   B. Murrain of beasts   C. Locusts   D. Frogs

139. What was the sixth plague?
    A. Flies   B. Boils   C. Frogs   D. Lice

140. What was the seventh plague?
    A. Hail   B. Lice   C. Mice   D. Locusts

141. What was the eighth plague?
    A. Locusts   B. Darkness   C. Pestilence   D. Flies

142. What was the ninth plague?
    A. Locusts   B. Flies   C. Frogs   D. Darkness

143. What feast began before the tenth plague?
    A. Pentecost   B. Passover   C. Thanksgiving   D. Firstfruits

144. What did Moses instruct the Israelites to put on their doors?
    A. A cross   B. Blood   C. Writing   D. A star

145. What was the tenth plague?
    A. Frogs   B. Death of the firstborn   C. A flood   D. Pestilence

146. Who killed the firstborn of man and beast?
    A. Moses   B. God   C. The death angel   D. Pharoah

147. What was the first month of the Hebrew year?
    A. January   B. Ab   C. Sivan   D. Abib

148. How many years were the Israelites in Egypt?
    A. 120   B. 430   C. 350   D. 505

149. Whose bones did the Israelites take with them when they left Egypt?
    A. Abraham's   B. Joseph's   C. Jacob's   D. Pharoah's

150. By day the Lord went before the Israelites in _____.
   A. A pillar of cloud   B. A pillar of fire
   C. A calf   D. Lightning

151. By night the Lord went before the Israelites in _____.
   A. A pillar of fire   B. A pillar of cloud
   C. Lightning   D. A calf

152. Who raised his rod and divided the Red Sea?
   A. Aaron   B. Pharoah   C. Gideon   D. Moses

153. Moses sang praises to God after their deliverance. Who danced?
   A. Aaron   B. Miriam   C. Joshua   D. Moses

154. What happened after the Israelites complained about having no food?
   A. Nothing   B. God sent manna   C. They went hungry
   D. They killed their cattle

155. When the people gathered more manna than they needed and it was
   left until morning, what happened to it?
   A. It vanished   B. Nothing   C. It had worms in it
   D. It turned black

156. What happened when people went to gather manna on the Sabbath?
   A. There was no manna   B. The manna was rancid
   C. There was double manna   D. They were struck by lightning

157. What did Moses tell Aaron to do with the manna?
   A. To put the manna in a pot   B. To eat the manna
   C. To give the manna to others   D. To destroy the manna

158. When the people were thirsty at Rephidim, what did God tell Moses
   to do?
   A. To hit a rock   B. To speak to the rock
   C. To drill a well   D. To hit a tree

159. Whom did Moses send to fight the Amalekites?
   A. Aaron   B. Joshua   C. Eleazar   D. Ithamar

160. During the battle with the Amalekites, what happened when Moses
   raised his arms?
   A. The Israelites lost   B. The Amalekites won
   C. The Israelites won   D. It was a tie

161. Who held up Moses' arms after Moses got tired of holding them up?
   A. Aaron and Miriam   B. Aaron and Hur
   C. Aaron and Joshua   D. Moses

162. Moses' sons were Gershom and who?
   A. Eliezer   B. Reuben   C. Pharex   D. Moses had just one son

163. After Jethro saw Moses judge the people, what advice did he give Moses?
   A. To appoint other judges   B. To judge not
   C. To leave the country
   D. To have the people solve their own problems

164. On what mount did Moses receive the Ten Commandmants?
   A. Mt. Sinai   B. Mt. Ararat   C. Mt. Olivet   D. Mt. Moriah

165. What is the first commandment?
   A. Thou shalt not make any graven image
   B. Honor thy father and thy mother
   C. Thou shalt have no other gods before me
   D. Thou shalt not kill

166. What is the second commandment?
   A. Thou shalt have no other gods before me
   B. Thou shalt not make any graven image
   C. Thou shalt not take the name of the Lord in vain
   D. Thou shalt not steal

167. What is the third commandment?
   A. Thou shalt not take the name of the Lord thy God in vain
   B. Thou shalt not make any graven image   C. Thou shalt not kill
   D. Thou shalt not steal

168. What is the fourth commandment?
   A. Thou shalt not covet
   B. Remember the Sabbath day to keep it holy
   C. Thou shalt not kill   D. Thou shalt not steal

169. What is the fifth commandment?
   A. Honor thy father and thy mother
   B. Thou shalt not make any graven image
   C. Thou shalt have no other gods before me
   D. Thou shalt not covet

170. What is the sixth commandment?
   A. Thou shalt not steal
   B. Thou shalt not take the name of the Lord thy God in vain
   C. Thou shalt not kill
   D. Thou shalt not bear false witness

171. What is the seventh commandment
   A. Thou shalt not commit adultery   B. Thou shalt not kill
   C. Thou shalt not steal
   D. Thou shalt not bear false witness

172. What is the eighth commandment
    A. Thou shalt not covet   B. Thou shalt not kill
    C. Honor thy father and thy mother   D. Thou shalt not steal

173. What is the ninth commandment?
    A. Thou shalt not covet
    B. Thou shalt not bear false witness
    C. Remember the Sabbath day to keep it holy
    D. Thou shalt not steal

174. What is the tenth commandment?
    A. Honor thy father and thy mother
    B. Thou shalt not steal
    C. Thou shalt not bear false witness
    D. Thou shalt not covet

175. How long was Moses on Mt. Sinai with the Lord?
    A. 40 hours   B. 40 days   C. 20 days   D. 35 days

176. What was to cover the mercy seat on the ark of the covenant?
    A. Seraphim   B. Cherubim   C. Horns   D. A rainbow

177. Who was the first high priest?
    A. Moses   B. Levi   C. Aaron   D. Joshua

178. Who were Aaron's sons?
    A. Gad, Naphtali, Issachar, and Levi
    B. Peter, Andrew, James, and John
    C. Nadab, Abihu, Eleazar, and Ithamar
    D. Shem, Ham, Japheth, and Amos

179. Who wrote God's laws on the two tables of stone?
    A. Aaron   B. Joshua   C. Moses   D. God

180. Who made the golden calf?
    A. Dathan   B. Aaron   C. Joshua   D. Moses

181. What did God want to do to the people after they rebelled?
    A. Nothing   B. Destroy them   C. Forgive them
    D. Forget about them

182. Why didn't God do as He planned?
    A. He forgave them instead
    B. Moses prayed that He would not do it
    C. The people asked for mercy
    D. Aaron prayed for the people

183. Who went down with Moses from Mt. Sinai?
    A. Aaron   B. God   C. No one   D. Joshua

184. Why did Moses break the two tables of stone?
A. He tripped and fell B. He was angry
C. He did not like them D. They were too heavy

185. What did Moses do with the golden calf?
A. Nothing B. He ground it into powder
C. He ignored it D. He threw it into the Red Sea

186. Moses wanted to see God, but God said Moses could not see

_____ .

A. His face B. His angels C. His feet D. His chariot

187. What happened to Moses' face when he was on the mount with God?
A. It shone B. It got darker C. Nothing D. It got hairier

188. What did Moses put over his face?
A. A mask B. Nothing C. A coat D. A veil

189. What did the people do if the cloud stayed on the tabernacle?
A. They moved B. They stayed
C. They looked at it D. They ignored it

190. What did the people do if the cloud lifted.
A. They stayed B. They looked at it
C. They became afraid D. They moved

191. God told Moses to count all the Israelites who were at least

_____ .

A. 16 B. 20 C. 21 D. 30

192. Which tribe was not counted?
A. Judah B. Dan C. Simeon D. Levi

193. Which tribe was in charge of caring for the tabernacle?
A. Benjamin B. Judah C. Levi D. Issachar

194. How many tribes camped on each side of the tabernacle?
A. 2 B. 4 C. 5 D. 3

195. Which of Aaron's sons died for offering wrongly?
A. Ithamar and Eleazar B. Nadab and Abihu
C. Joshua and Dan D. Nadab and Eleazar

196. What covered the tabernacle by day?
A. Fire B. Rain C. Clouds D. Darkness

197. What covered the tabernacle by night?
A. Fog B. Rain C. Fire D. Clouds

198. What did God send to supply the Israelites with meat?
A. Sheep B. Quail C. Oxen D. Camels

199. Why did Aaron and Miriam speak against Moses?
    A. He was becoming too strict
    B. He had married an Ethiopian
    C. He liked Joshua more   D. They wanted to be leaders

200. After God spoke with them, they discovered that Miriam had
    _____ .
    A. A golden ring   B. The Ten Commandments
    C. A scarlet robe   D. Leprosy

201. Who prayed that Miriam would be healed?
    A. Miriam   B. Moses   C. Aaron   D. All Israel

202. How long was Miriam required to be outside of the camp?
    A. 40 days   B. 7 days   C. 14 days   D. 1 year

203. How many men were sent to spy in the land of Canaan?
    A. 12   B. 2   C. 40   D. 21

204. What kind of food did the spies carry back on a staff?
    A. Grapes   B. Bananas   C. A calf   D. Apples

205. How many days did they spy in Canaan?
    A. 24   B. 12   C. 38   D. 40

206. What was unusual about the sons of Anak?
    A. They were dwarfs   B. They were giants
    C. They had blond hair   D. They were archers

207. How many spies thought the Israelites could not conquer the land?
    A. 6   B. 12   C. 2   D. 10

208. Which spies said that Israel could conquer the land?
    A. Moses and Aaron   B. Joshua and Caleb
    C. Dan and Bethel   D. Reuben and Simeon

209. After the Israelites refused to enter the land, what did God plan to do?
    A. Encourage them   B. Have the enemy attack
    C. Lead them in   D. Kill them

210. Why didn't God do as He planned?
    A. The Israelites repented   B. Moses prayed for Israel
    C. The Israelites went into the land
    D. Joshua prayed for the people

211. God said that the people _____ years old and up would die in the wilderness.
    A. 35   B. 40   C. 18   D. 20

212. Which two spies would be able to go into the Promised Land?
    A. Dan and Bethel   B. Joshua and Caleb
    C. Moses and Aaron   D. Aaron and Hur

213. How many years did the Israelites wander in the wilderness?
    A. 20   B. 10   C. 40   D. 35

214. God said they would wander in the wilderness one year for

    _____ .

    A. Each spy who rebelled against him
    B. Each day they refused to conquer the land
    C. Each day they had spied out the land
    D. Each elder of Israel

215. What happened to the ten spies who said they could not conquer the land?
    A. They were stoned to death
    B. They were banished from camp
    C. The Canaanites killed them
    D. They died in a plague

216. Korah, Dathan, and _____ started a rebellion against Moses.
    A. Aaron   B. Gedaliah   C. Gershom   D. Abiram

217. What happened to Korah, Dathan, and Abiram?
    A. The Lord struck them with lightning
    B. The earth opened up and they fell in
    C. The Amorites attracked and killed them
    D. They became the new leaders

218. Aaron's rod was chosen to represent _____ .
    A. Levi   B. Judah   C. Benjamin   D. Ephraim

219. What happened to Aaron's rod?
    A. It budded, blossomed, and yielded almonds
    B. It glowed with God's glory
    C. It became gold   D. It turned black

220. Where was Aaron's rod placed?
    A. In the temple   B. In the ark of the covenant
    C. In Moses' tent   D. It was buried on Mt. Sinai

221. Which relative of Moses died in Kadesh?
    A. Gershom   B. Miriam   C. Aaron   D. Jethro

222. When the Israelites needed water, what was Moses supposed to do to the rock?
    A. Hit the rock   B. Worship the rock
    C. Write upon the rock   D. Speak to it

223. What did Moses do to the rock?
    A. He covered it with his mantle   B. He hit it
    C. He spoke to the rock   D. He put blood upon the rock

224. Who did God say would not enter the Promised Land?
    A. Aaron   B. Joshua   C. Moses   D. Moses and Aaron

225. Where did Aaron die?
    A. Mt. Sinai   B. Mt. Ararat   C. Mt. Olivet   D. Mt. Hor

226. Who succeeded Aaron as high priest?
    A. Moses   B. Eleazar   C. Ithamar   D. Joshua

227. After the Israelites complained, what did God send upon them?
    A. Hail   B. Fire   C. A flood   D. Serpents

228. Moses made a serpent of brass. What did he do with it?
    A. He touched all the people who had been bitten
    B. He put it in the tabernacle.
    C. He began to worship it   D. He set it upon a pole

229. What did the people who had been bitten have to do with the brass
    serpent?
    A. Kiss it   B. Look at it   C. Touch it   D. Worship it

230. What king wanted Balaam to curse Israel?
    A. Pharoah   B. Achish   C. Jehu   D. Balak

231. What country did he rule?
    A. Edom   B. Moab   C. Ammon   D. Syria

232. What did Balaam's donkey see that made him stop?
    A. A wolf   B. An angel   C. A lion   D. A wall

233. After Balaam had beaten his donkey, what did the donkey do?
    A. It spoke   B. It bucked him off
    C. It turned and ran   D. It collapsed

234. Then what did Balaam see?
    A. An angel   B. A bright star
    C. The Israelites   D. A pillar of fire

235. How many times did Balaam try to curse Israel?
    A. 1   B. 6   C. 4   D. 3

236. Whom did God choose as Moses' successor?
    A. Joshua   B. Samuel   C. Eleazar   D. Ithamar

237. When the Israelites defeated Midian, what man did they kill?
    A. Og   B. Sihon   C. Balaam   D. Bashan

238. How old was Aaron when he died?
A. 123   B. 84   C. 120   D. 99

239. Where did the Israelites stand to hear God's blessings?
A. Mt. Ararat   B. Mt. Sinai   C. Mt. Ebal   D. Mt. Gerizim

240. Where did the Israelites stand to hear God's curse?
A. Mt. Ararat   B. Mt. Sinai   C. Mt. Ebal   D. Mt. Gerizim

241. God said that any king of Israel should not have much silver and gold, many wives, and many _____ .
A. Servants   B. Crowns   C. Enemies   D. Horses

242. From what mount did Moses view the Promised Land?
A. Mt. Hor   B. Mt. Sinai   C. Mt. Pisgah   D. Mt. Olivet

243. Where did Moses die?
A. Moab   B. Ammon   C. Syria   D. Israel

244. Who buried Moses?
A. Joshua   B. Eleazar   C. No one   D. God

245. How old was Moses when he died?
A. 120   B. 80   C. 96   D. 77

246. Who was Joshua's father?
A. Moses   B. Nadab   C. Nun   D. Jesse

247. Joshua sent two men to spy on _____ .
A. Jerusalem   B. Hebron   C. Gilgal   D. Jericho

248. At whose house did the two spies stay in Jericho?
A. Ruth's   B. Rahab's   C. Rachel's   D. Rezin's

249. What did Rahab ask the spies to do?
A. To take her back with them   B. Not to come back
C. To kill the king of Jericho
D. Not to kill her or her family

250. How did the spies get out of Jericho?
A. They disguised themselves
B. Rahab lowered them over a wall with a cord
C. They stole horses and rode out   D. They did not get out

251. What color was the cord?
A. Blue   B. Green   C. Scarlet   D. White

252. What was Rahab to do with the cord?
A. To lower herself down the wall
B. To tie it around her robes
C. To tie it in the window   D. To burn it

253. The Jordan River divided after who had stepped into its water?
    A. Joshua   B. The spies   C. Rahab   D. The priests

254. Joshua commanded the Israelites to take _____ stones out of the river.
    A. 40   B. 20   C. 3   D. 12

255. What did Joshua set up in the midst of the Jordan River?
    A. A wooden marker   B. Twelve stones
    C. His rod   D. The Ten Commandments

256. What did Joshua set up on Jordan's bank as a memorial?
    A. His rod   B. A wooden marker
    C. The Ten Commandments   D. Twelve stones

257. What feast did Israel observe at this time?
    A. Pentecost   B. Day of Atonement
    C. Feast of Tabernacles   D. Passover

258. What did God stop supplying once Israel entered the Promised Land?
    A. His protection   B. Manna   C. Quail   D. His guidance

259. As Israel marched around Jericho, what did the priests carry before the ark?
    A. Swords   B. Banners   C. Trumpets
    D. The Ten Commandments

260. How many times did Israel march around Jericho on the first day?
    A. Seven times   B. Three times   C. Twelve times   D. Once

261. How many days did Israel march around Jericho one time?
    A. 1   B. 5   C. 12   D. 6

262. How many times did Israel march around Jericho on the seventh day?
    A. 1   B. 3   C. 6   D. 7

263. When the priests blew their trumpets, what did Joshua tell the people to do?
    A. Charge   B. Shout   C. Fight   D. Retreat

264. What then happened to the people of Jericho?
    A. They defeated Israel   B. They surrendered to Israel
    C. They repented of their sins   D. Their walls fell down

265. Whose family was not killed?
    A. The king's   B. Rahab's   C. Rachel's   D. Jezebel's

266. After Jericho, what was the next city defeated by Israel?
    A. Gilgal   B. Jerusalem   C. Gibeon   D. Ai

267. What city craftily made a peace treaty with Israel?
    A. Ai   B. Gibeon   C. Hebron   D. Ramah

268. As Israel fought the confederacy of kings, how did God help them?
    A. He sent a great thunderstorm
    B. Lightning struck the enemy
    C. He struck the enemy blind
    D. Hailstones dropped on the enemy

269. In the same battle, what happened to the sun?
    A. It was covered with clouds
    B. It scorched the enemy with great heat
    C. It turned as red as blood   D. It did not go down

270. How long was the sun like this?
    A. Until the sixth hour   B. Until the ninth hour
    C. Until midnight   D. About one day

271. How many tribes settles on the east side of the Jordan River?
    A. 12   B. 4   C. 2½   D. 9½

272. Which tribe received no inheritance?
    A. Judah   B. Levi   C. Dan   D. Simeon

273. Who was Eleazar's son?
    A. Gershom   B. Phinehas   C. Joshua   D. Caleb

274. Who said, "But as for me and my house, we will serve the Lord"?
    A. Caleb   B. Moses   C. Eleazar   D. Joshua

275. How old was Joshua when he died?
    A. 110   B. 99   C. 90   D. 75

276. Whose bones were buried in Shechem?
    A Joseph's   B. Joshua's   C. Moses'   D. Caleb's

277. Who was the woman judge?
    A. Deborah   B. Dinah   C. Ruth   D. Elisabeth

278. Whom did she commission to lead Israel against Sisera?
    A. Barak   B. Balaam   C. Joab   D. Balak

279. Barak said he would go if Deborah would do something. What?
    A. Choose another leader   B. Go with him
    C. Marry him   D. Pray for him

280. After Sisera had fled to her tent, what woman killed him?
    A. Ruth   B. Deborah   C. Rahab   D. Jael

281. To whom did God's angel speak concerning Israel's deliverance from Midian?
    A. Joash   B. Gideon   C. Samuel   D. Joel

282. The first time Gideon put the fleece before the Lord, what did he want God to do to the fleece?
A. Make it brown   B. Make it wet
C. Set it on fire   D. Make it dry

283. What did Gideon want God to do to the fleece the second time?
A. Set it on fire   B. Make it dry
C. Make it brown   D. Make it wet

284. How many men were in Gideon's army?
A. 3,000   B. 330   C. 3,300   D. 300

285. Gideon gave each of his men a pitcher, a lamp, and a
_____ .

A. Sword   B. Spear   C. Trumpet   D. Map

286. Why did Jephthah's brothers reject him from sharing their inheritance?
A. His mother was a harlot   B. He was less cultured
C. He continually stirred up trouble
D. He had killed their father

287. Jephthah would fight the Ammonites if the elders of Gilead made him what?
A. A rich man   B. Captain   C. King   D. A new house.

288. Jephthah promised that if God helped defeat the Ammonites, he would _____ .
A. Sacrifice the first thing that came out of his house
B. Consecrate his son to the Lord
C. Pay twenty talents of silver to the Lord
D. Become king and faithfully follow God

289. When Jephthah returned from beating the Ammonites, who was the first to greet him?
A. His son   B. His daughter   C. His wife   D. His servant

290. After Jephthah defeated the Ephraimites, he caught those trying to escape when they mispronounced what word?
A. Jephthah   B. Jerusalem   C. Shibboleth   D. Shechem

291. Who was Manoah's son?
A. Samuel   B. Samson   C. Eli   D. David

292. Who told Manoah's wife that she would have a son?
A. Manoah   B. Samuel   C. God's angel   D. The Lord

293. What did the angel do when Manoah and his wife made an offering?
A. He set it on fire   B. He went to heaven in the flame
C. He rejected the offering   D. He ate it

294. What animal did Samson kill?
    A. A lion   B. A bear   C. An ox   D. A camel

295. A few days later what did Samson find in the carcass of the animal?
    A. Honey   B. Weeds   C. A rabbit   D. Gold

296. How did the young men discover the answer to Samson's riddle?
    A. Samson's wife told them   B. They just guessed
    C. They discovered the lion's carcass
    D. They could not answer the riddle

297. What did Samson do after he caught three hundred foxes?
    A. He made a coat for his wife   B. He let them go
    C. He made the Philistines eat them
    D. He tied their tails together

298. How many Philistines did Samson kill with the jawbone of an ass?
    A. 100   B. 500   C. 330   D. 1,000

299. After the Philistines had surrounded the city, how did Samson escape from Gaza?
    A. He disguised himself as a Philistine
    B. He hid himself in a straw wagon
    C. He carried the gates of the city on his back and left
    D. He escaped while the city was burning

300. With whom did Samson fall in love?
    A. Hannah   B. Delilah   C. Ruth   D. Rahab

301. When Delilah first asked Samson how he would lose his strength, what did he say?
    A. Cut his hair off   B. Tie him with seven green withs
    C. Get him drunk   D. Tie him with new ropes

302. When Delilah asked the second time, what did Samson say would take away his strength?
    A. To have his hair cut off
    B. To be tied with seven green withs
    C. To have his hair woven together
    D. To be tied with new ropes

303. What did Samson say when Delilah asked the third time?
    A. To have his hair woven together
    B. To be tied with new ropes
    C. To have his hair cut off
    D. To be tied with seven green withs

304. What did Samson say when Delilah asked the fourth time?
    A. To have his hair cut off
    B. To have his hair woven together
    C. To be tied with seven green withs
    D. To be tied with new ropes

305. Who cut off Samson's hair?
    A. His mother B. A man   C. Delilah   D. Samson

306. How many people were killed when Samson pulled the house down?
    A. 10,000   B. 3,000   C. 500   D. 150

307. Who was Elimelech's wife?
    A. Ruth   B. Orpah   C. Hannah   D. Naomi

308. What city was Elimelech from?
    A. Jerusalem   B. Shiloh   C. Gilgal   D. Bethlehem

309. Who were Elimelech's two sons?
    A. Eleazar and Phinehas   B. Mahlon and Chilion
    C. Joel and Abiah   D. James and John

310. When there was a famine in Judah, where did Elimelech's family move?
    A. Edom   B. Moab   C. Syria   D. Ammon

311. What were the names of Mahlon's and Chilion's wives?
    A. Ruth and Esther   B. Ruth and Orpha
    C. Mara and Orpah   D. Ruth and Naomi

312. After Elimelech, Mahlon, and Chilion died in Moab, who returned with Naomi to Bethlehem?
    A. Boaz   B. Orpah   C. Obed   D. Ruth

313. Naomi no longer wanted to be called Naomi but what?
    A. Mara   B. Hannah   C. Martha   D. Esther

314. In whose field did Ruth glean?
    A. Boaz's   B. David's   C. Mahlon's   D. Samuel's

315. Who married Ruth?
    A. Elimelech   B. Boaz   C. Eli   D. David

316. What was the name of Ruth's son?
    A. David   B. Obed   C. Samuel   D. Saul

317. What relation was Ruth to King David?
    A. Mother   B. Sister   C. Grandmother   D. Great-grandmother

318. Who was Hannah's husband?
    A. Elimelech   B. Elkanah   C. Eli   D. Abimelech

319. What did Hannah promise to give to the Lord?
    A. More money   B. Her son
    C. Her tithe   D. A burnt offering

320. Who was the priest that saw Hannah praying?
    A. Eleazar   B. Phinehas   C. Aaron   D. Eli

321. Eli could see Hannah's lips move but couldn't hear her, so he thought
    she _____ .
    A. Had laryngitis   B. Was drunk
    C. Was asleep   D. Was insincere

322. Who was Elkanah and Hannah's son?
    A. Samson   B. Saul   C. Samuel   D. Josiah

323. What did Hannah bring to Samuel every year?
    A. His allowance   B. His lunch
    C. New shoes   D. A new coat

324. Who were Eli's sons?
    A. Nadab and Abihu   B. Joel and Abiah
    C. Eleazar and Phinehas   D. Hophni and Phinehas

325. What was wrong with Eli's sons?
    A. They were very young   B. They were wicked
    C. They were incompetent   D. They were deformed

326. What did God's messenger say would happen to Eli's sons?
    A. They would repent
    B. They would die on the same day
    C. They would corrupt the people
    D. God would not honor them

327. Samuel heard someone call his name. He thought it was Eli, but who
    was it?
    A. Hannah   B. The Lord   C. Hophni   D. Elkanah

328. How many times did Samuel go to Eli, thinking he had called?
    A. 4   B. 2   C. 1   D. 3

329. What message did the Lord tell Samuel?
    A. That he would be priest
    B. That Eli's family would be punished
    C. That Samuel should return home
    D. That Samuel would be king

330. After Israel was beaten by the Philistines, what was brought out to
    help them?
    A. The cavalry   B. The ark of the covenant
    C. More men   D. A sacrifice

26

331. In the next battle Eli's sons were killed. What else happened?
   A. The ark was taken   B. Samuel was killed
   C. Jerusalem was burned   D. Shiloh was attacked

332. When the messenger told Eli the news, what happened?
   A. Eli fell backward and died   B. Eli wept bitterly
   C. Eli prayed   D. Eli offered a trespass offering to God

333. How long did the Philistines have the ark of the covenant?
   A. One year   B. Seven days   C. Seven weeks   D. Seven months

334. Samuel's sons were wicked and the people asked for

   _____ .

   A. New priests   B. A king   C. Lower taxes   D. A temple

335. Who was Saul's father?
   A. Abiah   B. Samuel   C. Josiah   D. Kish

336. Saul was from what tribe?
   A. Benjamin   B. Judah   C. Simeon   D. Ephraim

337. What was Saul sent out to find?
   A. Donkeys   B. Sheep   C. Money   D. Camels

338. A prophet used to be called a _____ .
   A. Fortune teller   B. Seer   C. Soothsayer   D. Magician

339. At Mizpeh, Saul was chosen king, but he was _____ .
   A. On his way to Mizpeh   B. Kidnapped
   C. Standing in the back   D. Hiding

340. Who was Saul's son?
   A. Joshua   B. Jonathan   C. Josiah   D. Joel

341. Who was Saul's captain?
   A. Joab   B. Amasa   C. Abner   D. Adonijah

342. God sent Samuel to Jesse's house which was in _____ .
   A. Jerusalem   B. Shiloh   C. Gilgal   D. Bethlehem

343. Which of Jesse's sons did Samuel anoint as king?
   A. Eliab   B. David   C. Shammah   D. Solomon

344. When Saul needed to be calmed, David would play _____
   for him.
   A. A trumpet   B. A harp   C. A guitar   D. Brahm's lullaby

345. Who was the Philistine giant that challenged Israel?
   A. Gath   B. Goliath   C. Gaza   D. Gerizim

346. Who killed the giant?
   A. Saul   B. Samuel   C. Jonathan   D. David

347. After the giant was killed, the women sang, "Saul hath slain his thousands, and David _____."
    A. Helped him B. His ten thousands
    C. Only one D. His thousands

348. Saul was jealous of David and threw _____ at him?
    A. A vase B. A javelin C. A sword D. A book

349. Who loved David "as his own soul"?
    A. Jonathan B. Saul C. Samuel D. Jesse

350. Which daughter of Saul did David marry?
    A. Michal B. Abigail C. Ahinoam D. Sheba

351. On a second occasion what did Saul throw at David?
    A. A sword B. A rock C. His armor D. A javelin

352. Who lowered David down through a window?
    A. Jonathan B. Michal C. Saul D. David himself

353. Who killed eighty-five priests at Saul's command?
    A. Doeg B. Jonathan C. David D. Abner

354. Who escaped and told David of the priests' deaths?
    A. Jael B. Joab C. Abiathar D. Abner

355. Who made a covenant with David?
    A. Jonathan B. Saul C. Samuel D. Joab

356. David cut off part of his robe, but spared his life. Whose life?
    A. Jonathan's B. Doeg's C. Saul's D. Abner's

357. To whom did David show the piece cut from the robe?
    A. Abner B. Joab C. Samuel D. Saul

358. Who died and was buried at Ramah?
    A. Saul B. David C. Samuel D. Michal

359. In Carmel, David's men asked for food from _____ .
    A. Shimei B. Eli C. Saul D. Nabal

360. Who was Nabal's wife?
    A. Ahinoam B. Esther C. Abigail D. Ruth

361. Who gave food to David so he would not attack?
    A. Abigail B. Nabal C. Jonathan D. Saul

362. What happened to Nabal a few days later?
    A. He left the country B. He joined David's men
    C. He died D. He was kidnapped

363. Who married Abigail?
    A. David B. Jonathan C. Saul D. Abner

364. Who went with David into Saul's camp?
    A. Abishai B. Abner C. Joab D. Ahimelech

365. What did Abishai want to do to Saul?
    A. Capture him B. Tie him up
    C. Leave him alone D. Kill him

366. What did David take from Saul?
    A. His sword B. His crown C. His spear and a cruse of water
    D. His robe

367. After taking them, to whom did David shout?
    A. Saul B. Joab C. Abner D. Abishai

368. Saul went to see a witch at _____ .
    A. Jerusalem B. Endor C. Gaza D. Hebron

369. Who did Saul want to see?
    A. Jonathan B. David C. Eli D. Samuel

370. What did Samuel tell Saul about his kingdom?
    A. It would be divided B. It would collapse
    C. It would last forever D. It would be given to David

371. What did Samuel tell Saul about Saul and his sons?
    A. They would rule forever B. They would be killed
    C. They would defeat the Philistines
    D. David would kill them

372. On what mount did Saul and his sons die?
    A. Mt. Sinai B. Mt. Gilboa C. Mt. Horeb D. Mt. Pisgah

373. Who killed Saul?
    A. His armorbearer B. David C. Saul D. The Philistines

374. After Saul's death, who killed himself?
    A. Jonathan B. David C. Saul's armorbearer D. Abner

375. What did the Philistines do with Saul's body?
    A. Left it B. Buried it
    C. Burned it D. Hung it on a wall

376. The men of what city rescued Saul's body?
    A. Hebron B. Gilgal C. Beersheba D. Jabesh-gilead

377. In what city was Saul buried?
    A. Jerusalem B. Jabesh C. Hebron D. Gath

378. What did the men of Judah do to David?
    A. Banished him from the land of Judah B. Made him king
    C. Asked him to fight the Philistines
    D. Punished him for killing Saul

379. Who led David's men?
A. Abner   B. Samuel   C. Amasa   D. Joab

380. How old was David when he began to reign?
A. 24   B. 30   C. 35   D. 40

381. How many years did he reign?
A. 25   B. 30   C. 35   D. 40

382. Who sent trees to build David's house?
A. Joab   B. Hiram   C. Shechem   D. Nathan

383. To what city did David bring the ark of the covenant?
A. Hebron   B. Joppa   C. Shechem   D. Jerusalem

384. What did David do that made his wife Michal mad?
A. He killed Saul's sons   B. He locked Michal up
C. He banished her
D. He danced before the ark of the covenant

385. What building did David desire to build?
A. His palace   B. A pyramid
C. A tabernacle   D. A temple

386. What prophet told David he could not build the temple?
A. Isaiah   B. Iddo   C. Jehu   D. Nathan

387. Why wasn't David allowed to build the temple?
A. He was too old   B. He was not a Levite
C. He was a man of war   D. He had no materials

388. From his rooftop David saw which woman bathing?
A. Ruth   B. Bathsheba   C. Hannah   D. Esther

389. Who was Bathsheba's husband?
A. Solomon   B. Joab   C. Absalom   D. Uriah

390. After David learned that Bathsheba was pregnant with his child, for whom did he send?
A. Nathan   B. Uriah   C. Joab   D. The priest

391. After David inquired about the battle, he sent Uriah home, hoping he would sleep with his wife, but where did Uriah sleep?
A. At an inn   B. At the door of the king's house
C. On a park bench   D. On the street

392. Who got Uriah drunk so that he would go home to his wife?
A. David   B. Uriah   C. Nathan   D. Bathsheba

393. David's letter told Joab to do what?
   A. To make sure Uriah was killed
   B. To quickly win the battle
   C. To come home immediately   D. To surrender

394. What did David do when he learned that Uriah had been killed?
   A. He had Joab killed   B. He declared a day of mourning
   C. He told Joab to surrender   D. He married Bathsheba

395. Whom did God send to reprove David for his adultery and murder?
   A. An angel   B. Nathan   C. Joab   D. Solomon

396. What did Nathan say that made David realize his sins were known?
   A. O ye cursed of Israel   B. Thou art the man
   C. Repent and be baptized   D. God is not mocked

397. What happened to David and Bathsheba's first child?
   A. He eventually became king   B. He died
   C. He was killed by Nathan
   D. He became a part of the genealogy of Christ

398. Who was David and Bathsheba's second son?
   A. Nathan   B. Solomon   C. Joel   D. Abiah

399. What did Nathan call Solomon?
   A. Solomon   B. Josiah   C. Saul   D. Jedidiah

400. Who conspired against David and attempted to take his kingdom?
   A. Absalom   B. Joab   C. Solomon   D. Joash

401. Who was Absalom's chief counselor?
   A. Ahithophel   B. Hushai   C. Nathan   D. Joab

402. Which counselor, who was loyal to David, stayed in Jerusalem after
   Absalom took over?
   A. Ahithophel   B. Abiathar   C. Hushai   D. Nadab

403. As David fled from Jerusalem, who cursed him and threw stones at
   him?
   A. Shimei   B. Nathan   C. Abner   D. Barzillai

404. What did David do to Shimei?
   A. Nothing   B. He had him killed
   C. He took him with them   D. He had his field burned

405. What did Ahithophel counsel Absalom to do?
   A. To make Solomon his advisor
   B. To immediately pursue David
   C. To build up his army
   D. To hire the Edomites to fight David

406. Whose advice did Absalom take?

    A. Ahithophel's   B. Solomon's   C. Hushai's   D. Nathan's

407. When Ahithophel learned that his counsel had not been taken, what did he do?

    A. He hanged himself   B. He cursed Absalom
    C. He joined David's men   D. He fled to Syria

408. What did David tell his men to do with Absalom?

    A. To kill him on sight   B. To throw him in prison
    C. To deal gently with him   D. To banish him

409. What happened to Absalom?

    A. He continued to rule over Israel
    B. His hair got caught in a tree
    C. He defeated David's men   D. He fled to Babylon

410. Who killed Absalom?

    A. Joab   B. He killed himself   C. David   D. Abishai

411. As David returned to Jerusalem, who met him on the way?

    A. Shimei   B. An angel   C. Bathsheba   D. Josiah

412. Whom did David bless because of his help?

    A. Shimei   B. Joab   C. Solomon   D. Barzillai

413. Who started a short-lived rebellion against David?

    A. Joab   B. Sheba   C.   Amasa   D. Asahel

414. Who killed Amasa?

    A. David   B. Nathan   C. Absalom   D. Joab

415. Who killed Sheba?

    A. Joab   B. The people of Abel   C. David   D. God

416. In various fights David's men killed some giants who were related to
    _____.

    A. Saul   B. Ezra   C. Goliath   D. Gath

417. One of these giants had an unusual deformity. What was it?

    A. One of his arms was shorter than the other
    B. He only had one eye
    C. He had a hump on his back
    D. He had six fingers on each hand and six toes on each foot

418. David displeased God by doing what with the people of Israel?

    A. He made some of them slaves   B. He numbered them
    C. He made them serve idols   D. He caused them to curse God

419. Whom did David place in charge of numbering the people?

    A. Solomon   B. Joab   C. Shimei   D. Nathan

420. Which prophet did God send to David?
    A. Iddo   B. Nathan   C. Jonah   D. Gad

421. One of the punishments God offered to David was seven years of

    _____.

    A. Fighting   B. Famine   C. Storms   D. Disease

422. Another punishment God offered David was three months of

    _____.

    A. Famine   B. Fleeing before his enemies
    C. Disease   D. Storms

423. The third punishment God offered David was three days of

    _____.

    A. Pestilence   B. Famine   C. Floods   D. Fighting

424. What punishment was sent?
    A. Pestilence   B. Fleeing before enemies
    C. Famine   D. Floods

425. David saw God's angel stop at whose threshingfloor?
    A. David's   B. Ziba's   C. Solomon's   D. Araunah's

426. What did David do to stop the pestilence?
    A. Set Jerusalem on fire   B. Sacrificed to God
    C. Destroyed all the idols   D. Put blood on the doorposts

427. What did Araunah offer to do for David?
    A. To fight in his army
    B. To sell the things necessary for a sacrifice
    C. To donate the things necessary for a sacrifice
    D. To offer the sacrifice himself

428. When David was very old, who was chosen to lie in bed with him to
    keep him warm?
    A. Abishag   B. Bathsheba   C. Abigail   D. Michal

429. Which of David's sons tried to take over the kingdom?
    A. Amnon   B. Nathan   C. Solomon   D. Adonijah

430. Whom did David choose as his successor?
    A. Adonijah   B. Joash   C. Solomon   D. Joab

431. Adonijah asked Bathsheba to speak to Solomon about

    _____.

    A. Marrying Abishag   B. A military position
    C. A loan   D. Buying some land

432. What did Solomon do to Adonijah?
    A. He gave him Abishag   B. He banished him
    C. He had him killed   D. He promoted him

433. What did Solomon do to Abiathar the priest?
   A. He promoted him to high priest   B. He had him killed
   C. He had him kidnapped   D. He banished him to Anathoth

434. What did Solomon do to Joab?
   A. He confirmed him as captain   B. He banished him to Syria
   C. He had him killed   D. He had him thrown into prison

435. What did Solomon do to Shimei?
   A. He had him imprisoned   B. He was banished to Egypt
   C. He gave him some land   D. He ordered him never to leave Jerusalem

436. What happened when Shimei left Jerusalem?
   A. He was killed   B. He was banished   C. He fled to Moab
   D. He was imprisoned

437. Whom did Solomon marry?
   A. Pharoah's daughter   B. Abishag   C. Bathsheba   D. Abigail

438. What did Solomon ask from God?
   A. A long life   B. An understanding heart
   C. Gold   D. Many wives

439. What else did God give to Solomon?
   A. Many wives   B. Many horses
   C. Riches, honor, and long life   D. Syria

440. When two women argued that each was the true mother of a baby,
   what did Solomon say to do with the baby?
   A. To divide it in half   B. To give it to the first woman
   C. To give it to the second woman   D. To keep it himself

441. Which woman was given the baby?
   A. The one who defended the baby   B. Neither one
   C. The one who agreed to divide the baby   D. Both of them

442. How many proverbs did Solomon write?
   A. 3,000   B. 157   C. 1,500   D. 2,000

443. How many songs did Solomon write?
   A. 1,200   B. 1,005   C. 177   D. 3,200

444. To whom did Solomon send for trees?
   A. Asaph   B. Edom   C. Hiram   D. Shimei

445. What kind of trees did Solomon want?
   A. Oak   B. Cedar   C. Palm   D. Walnut

446. What country did these trees come from?
   A. Syria   B. Sinai   C. Ptolemy   D. Lebanon

447. What did Solomon give Hiram in return?
    A. Ivory   B. Gold   C. Horses   D. Wheat and oil

448. Solomon began to build the temple _____ years after the Israelites had left Egypt.
    A. 400   B. 480   C. 530   D. 700

449. After Solomon's prayer at the temple dedication, what happened to the sacrifice?
    A. Fire from heaven consumed it   B. The priests ate it
    C. Nothing   D. It was left for the birds of the air

450. How many years did it take to build Solomon's house?
    A. 1   B. 6   C. 9   D. 13

451. What queen came to see Solomon?
    A. Cleopatra   B. The queen of Sheba   C. Esther
    D. The queen of Egypt

452. Who succeeded Solomon as king?
    A. Josiah   B. Hosea   C. Rehoboam   D. Asa

453. Whom did the northern tribes of Israel choose for their king?
    A. Rehoboam   B. Saul   C. Jeroboam   D. Ahab

454. What did Jeroboam set up for the people to worship?
    A. Two golden bears   B. Two golden wolves
    C. Two golden lions   D. Two golden calves

455. In what cities did he set these up?
    A. Dan and Beersheba   B. Jerusalem and Shiloh
    C. Bethel and Dan   D. Shechem and Gad

456. What did Omri call the capital city he built?
    A. Samaria   B. Jerusalem   C. Omri   D. Bethel

457. Hiel rebuilt Jericho and fulfilled whose prophecy?
    A. Joshua's   B. Joseph's   C. Abraham's   D. Moses'

458. Who was Ahab's wife?
    A. Esther   B. Athaliah   C. Jezebel   D. Joanna

459. Elijah told Ahab that there wouldn't be _____.
    A. Rain   B. War   C. Peace   D. Judgment

460. What fed Elijah when he was by the brook Cherith?
    A. Ravens   B. Doves   C. Owls   D. Pigeons

461. At Zarephath, who did Elijah meet?
    A. Ahab   B. A widow   C. Elisha   D. An angel

462. Elijah told the widow that her meal and oil would last until God sent
_____.
A. Peace   B. The Messiah   C. Rain   D. Prosperity

463. Whose son did Elijah raise to life?
A. His own son   B. The widow's son   C. Ahab's son
D. The Syrian's son

464. Where did Elijah challenge the prophets of Baal?
A. Mt. Sinai   B. Mt. Olivet   C. Mt. Ararat   D. Mt. Carmel

465. How many prophets of Baal were there?
A. 450   B. 225   C. 76   D. 505

466. Whose sacrifice was consumed by fire?
A. Baal's prophets'   B. Ahab's   C. Elijah's   D. Omri's

467. What happened to the prophets of Baal?
A. They were killed   B. They were thrown into the sea
C. Nothing   D. They served in Ahab's palace

468. What did Elijah pray for?
A. Mercy   B. Patience   C. Rain   D. Strength

469. Who swore to kill Elijah?
A. Elisha   B. Ahab   C. Jehu   D. Jezebel

470. As Elijah fled, under what kind of tree did he rest?
A. Cedar   B. Oak   C. Juniper   D. Sycamore

471. An angel caused Elijah to eat and drink and then Elijah did not eat
for _____ days.
A. 3   B. 7   C. 20   D. 40

472. As the Lord passed by Elijah, what was the Lord in?
A. Wind   B. Earthquake   C. Fire   D. A still small voice

473. Whom was Elijah to anoint as a prophet?
A. Amos   B. Elisha   C. Jonah   D. Nahum

474. The Lord told Elijah that there were _____ in Israel who
had not served idols.
A. 70   B. 700   C. 7,000   D. 70,000

475. Whom did Jezebel have killed so Ahab could have his vineyard?
A. Nabal   B. Naboth   C. Naaman   D. Nadab

476. What happened when Elijah hit the Jordan River with his mantle?
A. Nothing   B. His mantle got wet
C. He could walk on the water   D. The Jordan River divided

477. What did Elisha want from Elijah?
    A. A double portion of his spirit   B. His mantle
    C. Elijah's scrolls   D. Elijah's staff

478. What did Elisha have to do to get what he wanted?
    A. Pray   B. Sacrifice four oxen to God
    C. Watch as Elijah went up into heaven
    D. Bow before Elijah

479. How did Elijah go up into heaven?
    A. By a whirlwind   B. He was suddenly lifted up
    C. Two angels took him   D. By a cloud

480. What did Elisha do with Elijah's mantle?
    A. He buried it   B. He burnt it upon the altar
    C. He parted the Jordan River   D. He threw it into the Jordan River

481. What did Elisha pour into the waters of Jericho?
    A. Oil   B. Water from the Jordan River   C. Meal   D. salt

482. What did Elisha tell the widow to do with her one pot of oil?
    A. Sell it   B. Pour it into the borrowed pots
    C. Use as little as possible
    D. Pour it on the ground

483. What did the Shunammite woman have built for Elisha?
    A. A house   B. A tent   C. A stable   D. A room

484. Who was Elisha's servant?
    A. Gaza   B. Gehazi   C. Baruch   D. Barak

485. What did Elisha pour into the pot of poisoned food?
    A. Water   B. Oil   C. Meal   D. Salt

486. Naaman was the captain of the army of what country?
    A. Israel   B. Judah   C. Syria   D. Assyria

487. From what disease did Naaman suffer?
    A. Dropsy   B. Paralysis   C. Blindness   D. Leprosy

488. To whom did he go to be healed?
    A. Elijah   B. Gehazi   C. Baruch   D. Elisha

489. What did Elisha tell him to do to be cured?
    A. To climb Mt. Sinai   B. To fight the Assyrians
    C. To wash seven times in the Jordan River   D. To pray

490. At first Naaman refused. Who persuaded him to wash?
    A. His servants   B. Gehazi   C. Elisha   D. The king of Syria

491. What happened when Naaman washed in the Jordan River?
    A. Nothing   B. His servants laughed
    C. He was healed   D. Elisha told him he needed faith

492. Elisha refused Naaman's gifts, but who secretly accepted them?
    A. Gehazi   B. Baruch   C. Elijah   D. Naaman's servants

493. What was his punishment?
    A. Naaman killed him   B. He was struck blind
    C. He could no longer walk   D. He got Naaman's leprosy

494. How did Elisha recover an ax head which had fallen into the river?
    A. He made the ax head float   B. It was lost forever
    C. He reached into the water and grabbed it
    D. He dove in and found it

495. What happened when a dead body was thrown into Elisha's grave?
    A. Nothing   B. The tomb collapsed
    C. The body became alive   D. It vanished

496. Which nation conquered Israel?
    A. Assyria   B. Babylon   C. Syria   D. Egypt

497. Who was Assyria's captain?
    A. Nebuchadnezzar   B. Rezin   C. Shallum   D. Rabshakeh

498. When Assyria threatened Judah, to what prophet did Hezekiah go?
    A. Elisha   B. Isaiah   C. Jeremiah   D. Amos

499. How many Assyrians did the angel of the Lord kill?
    A. 100,000   B. 10,500   C. 70,000   D. 185,000

500. Hezekiah was near death, but God extended his life for how many years?
    A. 5   B. 15   C. 3   D. 23

501. What sign from the sundial did Hezekiah ask for?
    A. That the sundial would topple over
    B. That the shadow would go forward ten degrees
    C. That there would be no shadow on the sundial
    D. That the shadow would go back ten degrees

502. Hezekiah showed all his possessions to men from what country?
    A. Assyria   B. Babylon   C. Egypt   D. Moab

503. What was found while the temple was being repaired?
    A. The lost treasury   B. A dead body
    C. The ark of the covenant   D. The book of the law

504. What Babylonian king captured Jerusalem?
    A. Nebuchadnezzar   B. Cyrus   C. Darius   D. Nebuzaradan

505. The people killed Gedaliah, the governor, and fled to
_____.

A. Babylon   B. Egypt   C. Edom   D. Syria

506. What king allowed the Jews to return to their homeland?
A. Nebuchadnezzar   B. Saul   C. Cyrus   D. Nimrod

507. Who was the leader of the priests?
A. Jeshua   B. Obed   C. Eli   D. Jehoida

508. Who was the leader of the people?
A. Zechariah   B. Cyrus   C. Daniel   D. Zerubbabel

509. What two prophets urged the people to rebuild the temple?
A. Ezra and Nehemiah   B. Hosea and Micah
C. Haggai and Zechariah   D. Zephaniah and Joel

510. What was Ezra's occupation?
A. Soldier   B. King   C. Scribe   D. Butler

511. What had the people done that greatly upset Ezra?
A. They had married foreigners
B. They had worshiped idols
C. They had burned the book of the law
D. They had cursed Ezra

512. Nehemiah served in a palace in what city?
A. Babylon   B. Persia   C. Shushan   D. Damascus

513. What was Nehemiah's occupation?
A. Soldier   B. Priest   C. Levite   D. The king's cupbearer

514. What king did Nehemiah serve?
A. Artaxerxes   B. Xerxes   C. Cyrus   D. David

515. What did Nehemiah request from the king?
A. Higher wages   B. A white horse
C. A better job   D. To go to Jerusalem

516. Who was Nehemiah's chief opponent?
A. Ezra   B. Ezekiel   C. Sanballat   D. Daniel

517. How long did it take to complete Jerusalem's wall?
A. 33 days   B. 52 days   C. 91 days   D. 13 months

518. Who was king during Esther's time?
A. Cyrus   B. Darius   C. Ahasuerus   D. Shallum

519. Over how many provinces did he rule?
A. 53   B. 77   C. 127   D. 183

520. In what city was the palace located?
    A. Damascus   B. Jerusalem   C. Persepolis   D. Shushan

521. Who was Ahasuerus' queen?
    A. Ruth   B. Rachel   C. Drusilla   D. Vashti

522. The king deposed Vashti as queen when she refused to do what?
    A. Leave the room   B. Come to him
    C. Stop talking   D. Take care of their son

523. Who was chosen as the new queen?
    A. Rahab   B. Esther   C. Sheba   D. Dinah

524. What was Esther's other name?
    A. Hannah   B. Hadassah   C. Hagar   D. Haran

525. Who had raised Esther?
    A. Haman   B. Ahasuerus   C. Vashti   D. Mordecai

526. What relation was Mordecai to Esther?
    A. Father   B. Cousin   C. Uncle   D. No relation

527. Who learned of a plot against King Ahasuerus?
    A. Haman   B. Mordecai   C. Esther   D. Vashti

528. To whom did Mordecai reveal the plot?
    A. Esther   B. Haman   C. Ahasuerus   D. Vashti

529. Whom did King Ahasuerus promote?
    A. Haman   B. Vashti   C. Esther   D. Ezra

530. Who refused to bow to Haman?
    A. Esther   B. Vashti   C. Arioch   D. Mordecai

531. Haman conspired to kill what group of people?
    A. Persians   B. Jews   C. Syrians   D. Samaritans

532. Before an uninvited visitor could see the king, the king had to hold what out?
    A. His hand   B. His crown   C. His robe   D. His sceptre

533. Who said, "If I perish, I perish"?
    A. Vashti   B. Esther   B. Haman   D. Mordecai

534. Whom did Esther invite to her banquet?
    A. The royal court   B. Haman and Mordecai
    C. Vashti and Haman   D. Ahasuerus and Haman

535. What was Esther's request at the banquet?
    A. To promote Mordecai
    B. For them to attend another banquet
    C. To stop killing the Jews   D. To promote Haman

536. Who was Haman's wife?
    A. Vashti B. Esther C. Zoar D. Zeresh

537. What did Haman's wife advise him to build?
    A. A new house B. A gallows
    C. New stables D. A high tower

538. Why did the king bestow honor on Mordecai?
    A. For being Esther's cousin B. For fighting bravely
    C. For revealing an assassination plot
    D. For showing the king how to save money

539. Who paraded Mordecai through the streets?
    A. Ahasuerus B. Esther C. Haman D. Ezra

540. At the next banquet, what was Esther's request?
    A. To be seated by the king B. To promote Haman
    C. To promote Mordecai
    D. To save the Jews from being killed

541. What happened to Haman?
    A. He was promoted B. He was exiled
    C. He was imprisoned D. He was killed

542. Who took Haman's place?
    A. Esther B. Zeresh C. Ahasuerus D. Mordecai

543. What happened to the Jews on the day they were to be killed?
    A. Nothing B. The Jews were killed
    C. The Jews were imprisoned
    D. The Jews killed their opponents

544. What holiday was instituted to recall the saving of the Jews?
    A. Hanukkah B. Purim C. Easter D. Christmas

545. Where did Job live?
    A. Ur B. Uz C. Uriah D. Urim

546. On the day that the sons of God came before the Lord, who else came?
    A. Job B. Satan C. Bildad D. Amram

547. God allowed Satan to touch Job's possessions, but he was forbidden to touch who?
    A. God B. Elihu C. Zophar D. Job

548. Job's children, camels, sheep, oxen, and donkeys were lost in how many days?
    A. 12 B. 1 C. 3 D. 8

549. When God allowed Satan to touch Job, what was he forbidden to do?
    A. Make him sick   B. Give him dreams
    C. Make him curse God   D. Kill him

550. What did Job have all over his body?
    A. Skin   B. Boils   C. Leprosy   D. Bruises

551. Who advised Job to "curse God and die"?
    A. Satan   B. His son   C. Elihu   D. His wife

552. Who were Job's three friends?
    A. Elihu, Samuel, and Jehu
    B. Eliphaz, Bildad, and Zophar
    C. Eliphaz, Elihu, and Bildad
    D. Baalam, Zophar, and Amos

553. When Job's friends came, no one spoke for how many days?
    A. 1   B. 3   C. 7   D. 10

554. The Lord answered Job out of what?
    A. Fire   B. Earthquake   C. Cloud   D. Whirlwind

555. Who was to pray for Job's friend?
    A. Elihu   B. Job   C. The Lord   D. Satan

556. The Lord gave Job how much more than he had before?
    A. Half as much   B. Twice as much
    C. Ten times more   D. Twenty times more

557. Who wrote the Psalms?
    A. Samuel   B. David   C. Eli   D. Solomon

558. "My cup runneth over" is found in which Psalm?
    A. Psalm 100   B. It is not in Psalms   C. Psalm 2   D. Psalm 23

559. Who wrote the Proverbs?
    A. David   B. Solomon   C. Ezekiel   D. Rehoboam

560. "The _____ is the beginning of wisdom."
    A. Curious mind   B. Fear of the Lord
    C. Asking of questions   D. Word of God

561. "A _____ answer turneth away wrath."
    A. Soft   B. Wise   C. Hasty   D. Witty

562. Some of the Proverbs were not written by Solomon but by
    _____ .
    A. Lemuel   B. Rehoboam   C. Samuel   D. Eli

563. What is the repeated saying in Ecclesiastes?
    A. Praise the Lord!   B. Beware of false prophets
    C. Mind the law   D. Vanity of vanities

564. "To everything there is a _____ , and a time to every purpose under the heaven."
A. Reason   B. Season   C. Plan   D. God

565. "And they shall beat their swords into _____."
A. Spears   B. Dust   C. Sickles   D. Plowshares

566. Isaiah saw God on the throne in the year _____ died.
A. Uzziah   B. Solomon   C. Jotham   D. Nebuchadnezzar

567. How many wings did the seraphim have?
A. 2   B. 4   C. 6   D. 8

568. "Behold, a virgin shall conceive, and bear a son, and shall call his name _____ ."
A. Immanuel   B. Christ   C. Messiah   D. Isaiah

569. Who was Isaiah's son?
A. Zebulun   B. Zechariah
C. Maher-shalal-hash-baz   D. Amoz

570. Isaiah 53 speaks of Christ's _____ .
A. Birth   B. Resurrection   C. Sufferings   D. Ascension

571. Jeremiah told the people that they would live by what?
A. Fighting   B. Faith   C. Surrendering   D. Fleeing

572. Jeremiah predicted the captivity would last _____ years.
A. 70   B. 2   C. 7   D. 33

573. Who wrote for Jeremiah, as Jeremiah spoke?
A. Barak   B. Balaam   C. Baruch   D. Baal

574. Jeremiah was accused of what crime?
A. Murder   B. Treason   C. Stealing   D. Adultery

575. What did the princes do with Jeremiah?
A. Killed him   B. Released him
C. Banished him   D. Imprisoned him

576. Jeremiah was forced to go to what country?
A. Babylon   B. Syria   C. Persia   D. Egypt

577. Who wrote Lamentations?
A. Isaiah   B. Jeremiah   C. Ezekiel   D. Daniel

578. Ezekiel saw visions while he was by what river?
A. Nile   B. Jordan   C. Chebar   D. Arnon

579. What was Ezekiel's occupation?
A. Scribe   B. King   C. Priest   D. Craftsman

580. By what title is Ezekiel referred to?
   A. Son of perdition   B. Son of God
   C. Son of shame   D. Son of man

581. What was Ezekiel commanded to eat?
   A. Honey   B. Locusts   C. Shewbread   D. A book

582. The Lord brought Ezekiel to a valley full of _____ .
   A. Wheat   B. Bones   C. Locusts   D. Rivers

583. What king took Daniel to Babylon?
   A. Josiah   B. David   C. Zedekiah   D. Nebuchadnezzar

584. What was Daniel renamed?
   A. Adam   B. Belteshazzar   C. Baruch   D. Belshazzar

585. Daniel's friends, Hananiah, Mishael, and Azariah, were renamed what?
   A. Eliphaz, Bildad, and Zophar   B. Jacob, Esau, and Asa
   C. Elihu, Bildad, and Jael
   D. Shadrach, Meshach, and Abednego

586. Nebuchadnezzar dreamed of a statue whose head was made of

   _____ .
   A. Silver   B. Brass   C. Iron   D. Gold

587. Nebuchadnezzar's statue had arms made of _____ .
   A. Brass   B. Silver   C. Gold   D. Iron

588. Nebuchadnezzar's statue had a belly made of _____ .
   A. Gold   B. Iron   C. Silver   D. Brass

589. Nebuchadnezzar's statue had legs made of _____ .
   A. Silver   B. Iron   C. Brass   D. Gold

590. Nebuchadnezzar's statue had feet made of iron and

   _____ .
   A. Brass   B. Mire   C. Gold   D. Clay

591. What broke Nebuchadnezzar's statue?
   A. An earthquake   B. A stone   C. Fire   D. A whirlwind

592. What did Nebuchadnezzar set up in Dura?
   A. A palace   B. A tower   C. An image   D. A prison

593. What were the people commanded to do when the music started?
   A. To dance   B. To turn around   C. To bow down   D. To hide

594. Who didn't bow down before Nebuchadnezzar's image?
   A. Shadrach   B. Meshach   C. Abednego   D. All of the above

595. What happened to them?

A. They were killed   B. They were imprisoned

C. They were promoted

D. They were thrown into the fiery furnace

596. What happened to the guards who threw them into the furnace?

A. The king killed them   B. The fire killed them

C. They fell into the furnace   D. They were promoted

597. Nebuchadnezzar saw four people in the furnace. Whom did he say the fourth person looked like?

A. A guard   B. The Son of God   C. Daniel   D. A lion

598. What did Nebuchadnezzar tell Shadrach, Meshach, and Abednego to do?

A. To fan themselves   B. To come out of the furnace

C. To stay in the furnace   D. To pray to his god

599. What did Nebuchadnezzar do to them when they came out?

A. Imprisoned them   B. Threw them into the lions' den

C. Banished them   D. Promoted them

600. Who saw the handwriting on the wall?

A. Nebuchadnezzar   B. Belshazzar   C. Cyrus   D. Darius

601. Who interpreted the handwriting on the wall?

A. Shadrach   B. Daniel   C. Cyrus   D. Belshazzar

602. What happened to Belshazzar that night?

A. He was killed   B. He was imprisoned

C. He was exiled   D. He fled to Egypt

603. Who was the king after Belshazzar?

A. Darius   B. Daniel   C. Nebuchadnezzar   D. Josiah

604. Who was thrown into the lions' den?

A. Shadrach   B. Meshach   C. Abednego   D. Daniel

605. Why was Daniel thrown into the lions' den?

A. For murder   B. For praying

C. For treason   D. For stealing

606. Who had shut the lions' mouths?

A. Daniel   B. The king   C. Meshach   D. An angel

607. What happened to Daniel's accusers?

A. They were exiled

B. They were thrown into the lions' den

C. They fled to Syria   D. They were promoted

608. Who was Hosea's wife?
    A. Esther   B. Hanani   C. Sheba   D. Gomer

609. "For they have sown the wind, and they shall reap the
    _____ ."
    A. Harvest   B. Reward   C. Whirlwind   D. Consequences

610. What was Amos' occupation?
    A. Baker   B. Scribe   C. Shepherd   D. Craftsman

611. Amos said there would be a famine, not of bread, but of what?
    A. The joy of the Lord   B. Peace in the valley
    C. Meat   D. Hearing the words of the Lord

612. The theme of Obadiah is the judgment of what country?
    A. Israel   B. Judah   C. Babylon   D. Edom

613. Who was Jonah's father?
    A. Amoz   B. Amram   C. Amalek   D. Amittai

614. God told Jonah to go to _____ .
    A. Jerusalem   B. Nineveh   C. Damascus   D. Samaria

615. But Jonah decided to go to _____ .
    A. Nineveh   B. Tarshish   C. Jericho   D. Jerusalem

616. Jonah boarded a ship in _____ .
    A. Nineveh   B. Joppa   C. Mt. Carmel   D. Jericho

617. What method did the sailors use to find the cause of the storm?
    A. They looked at the stars   B. They looked at the sun
    C. They drew signs   D. They cast lots

618. What did the sailors do with Jonah?
    A. Threw him overboard
    B. Put him in the hold of the ship
    C. Put him in the lifeboat   D. Strangled him

619. What swallowed Jonah?
    A. A great fish   B. The waves
    C. An octopus   D. A great white shark

620. How long was Jonah in the fish?
    A. One day   B. Three days   C. Seven days   D. Ten days

621. How did Jonah get out of the big fish?
    A. He swam out   B. The fish vomited him out
    C. The sailors came in and got him
    D. He did not get out

622. Jonah preached that in _____ days Nineveh would be overthrown.
    A. One hundred and twenty   B. Many   C. The last   D. Forty

623. What did the Ninevites do?
   A. They stoned Jonah   B. They fasted
   C. They prayed to their idols   D. They ignored Jonah

624. Did God destroy Nineveh in forty days?
   A. Partially   B. Yes   C. Completely   D. No

625. How many people lived in Nineveh?
   A. 30,000   B. 120,000   C. 234,000   D. 500,000

626. Micah predicted that Christ would be born where?
   A. Jerusalem   B. Jericho   C. Bethlehem   D. Shiloh

627. Nahum prophesied against what city?
   A. Damascus   B. Babylon   C. Nineveh   D. Jerusalem

628. God told Habakkuk that He would send what nation to punish the Jews?
   A. Assyrians   B. Romans   C. Egyptians   D. Chaldeans

629. Haggai urged the people to continue building _____ .
   A. The walls of Jerusalem   B. Their houses
   C. Their idols   D. The temple

630. Malachi told the people that they had robbed God by not doing what?
   A. Honoring their parents
   B. Paying their tithes and offerings
   C. Offering their sacrifices
   D. Keeping the sabbath holy

631. Who was Zacharias' wife?
   A. Anna   B. Mary   C. Phanuel   D. Elisabeth

632. Who told Zacharias that he and Elisabeth would have a son?
   A. Elisabeth   B. An angel   C. Mary   D. Joseph

633. What was the angel's name?
   A. Micah   B. Gabriel   C. Michael   D. Lucifer

634. Zacharias was unable to do what until after his son was born?
   A. Speak   B. Hear   C. Walk   D. Sleep

635. Who was Zacharias' son?
   A. John the Baptist   B. Simeon   C. Justus   D. Levi

636. Who was Jesus' mother?
   A. Martha   B. Mary   C. Sarah   D. Elisabeth

637. Who was Mary's husband?
   A. Zacharias   B. Joseph   C. John   D. Peter

638. What angel appeared to Mary?
A. Michael   B. Lucifer   C. Malachi   D. Gabriel

639. What was the relationship between Mary and Elisabeth?
A. Elisabeth was Mary's mother   B. They were cousins
C. Elisabeth was Mary's aunt
D. Elisabeth was Mary's grandmother

640. When Joseph knew that Mary was pregnant, what did he decide to do?
A. Marry her   B. Have her stoned   C. Take her to Egypt
D. Put her away privately

641. Who convinced Joseph to take Mary as his wife?
A. Mary   B. An angel   C. Jesus   D. Mary's mother

642. What does Immanuel mean?
A. What hath God wrought   B. God with us
C. The Word of God   D. The King of Israel

643. From what great king was Joseph descended?
A. Nebuchadnezzar   B. David   C. Saul   D. Caesar

644. Who decreed that all the world would be taxed?
A. Herod   B. Caesar Augustus   C. Pilate   D. Agrippa

645. Who was governor of Syria when Jesus was born?
A. Simeon   B. Cyrenius   C. Pilate   D. Zacharias

646. From what city did Joseph and Mary come?
A. Bethlehem   B. Nazareth   C. Jerusalem   D. Capernaum

647. To what city did Joseph and Mary go?
A. Jerusalem   B. Jericho   C. Nazareth   D. Bethlehem

648. Where was Jesus born?
A. Bethlehem   B. Jerusalem   C. Nazareth   D. Caesarea

649. In what country was Bethlehem?
A. Judea   B. Samaria   C. Galilee   D. Pontus

650. Who was king over Judea when Jesus was born?
A. Pilate   B. Festus   C. Agrippa   D. Herod

651. Where was the baby Jesus laid?
A. In a room   B. In a manger   C. In a window
D. On the floor

652. How many angels spoke to the shepherds?
A. One   B. Forty   C. Three   D. A multitude

653. Who said, "Glory to God in the highest"?
    A. The angels   B. The shepherds   C. Mary   D. Joseph

654. Where did the shepherds go, after the angels left?
    A. Jerusalem   B. Nazareth   C. Bethany   C. Bethlehem

655. How many days old was Jesus when he was circumcised?
    A. Two   B. Eight   C. Twelve   D. Twenty-one

656. Who came from the east to see Jesus?
    A. Simeon   B. The wise men   C. The shepherds   D. Anna

657. How many wise men came to see Jesus?
    A. Two   B. Four   C. The Bible doesn't say   D. Three

658. What had led the wise men?
    A. A star   B. An Arab guide   C. The sun   D. Their instincts

659. What Old Testament prophet predicted Christ would be born in Bethlehem?
    A. Zechariah   B. Malachi   C. Amos   D. Micah

660. Herod told the wise men to return and tell him where the Christ child was so Herod could _____.
    A. Worship Him   B. Kill Him   C. Give Him a gift
    D. Make Him king

661. The wise men's gifts were gold, frankincense, and _____.
    A. Silver   B. Jewels   C. Myrrh   D. Pearls

662. Who warned the wise men not to return to Herod?
    A. An angel   B. Joseph   C. Mary   D. God

663. Where did the angel tell Joseph to take his family?
    A. Jerusalem   B. Bethlehem   C. Egypt   D. Samaria

664. What did Herod do to the children of Bethlehem who were two or younger?
    A Gave them a party   B. Brought them to Jerusalem
    C. Nothing   D. Killed them

665. After Herod died, who told Joseph to return to Israel?
    A. No one   B. Mary   C. An angel   D. Jesus

666. Who ruled after Herod?
    A. Pilate   B. Philip   C. Agrippa   D. Archelaus

667. Where did Joseph and his family live?
    A. Capernaum   B. Jerusalem   C. Nazareth   D. Bethlehem

668. God said who would not die until he had seen Christ?
    A. Zacharias   B. Simeon   C. Joseph   D. John the Baptist

669. What elderly woman saw Christ at the temple?
A. Mary   B. Anna   C. Hannah   D. Elisabeth

670. To what town did Mary, Joseph, and Jesus go after they left the temple?
A. Bethlehem   B. Nazareth   C. Jerusalem   D. Shiloh

671. How old was Jesus when He went up to the feast at Jerusalem?
A. Sixteen   B. Eight   C. Ten   D. Twelve

672. Where did Mary and Joseph find Jesus?
A. At His aunt's   B. In the temple   C. In a stable   D. At home

673. Who said, "Wist ye not that I must be about my Father's business?"
A. Mary   B. Jesus   C. Joseph   D. John

674. Who was described as the "voice of one crying in the wilderness"?
A. John the Baptist   B. Simon Peter   C. Jesus   D. Zacharias

675. What did John the Baptist call the Pharisees and Sadducees?
A. Locusts   B. Rabbis   C. Vipers   D. Dogs

676. John the Baptist said that the Messiah would baptize with what?
A. Holy Ghost and fire   B. Water   C. Power   D. Judgment

677. Who baptized Jesus?
A. No one   B. Peter   C. Philip   D. John the Baptist

678. The Spirit of God descended in the form of a what?
A. Dove   B. Fire   C. Olive branch   D. Cloud

679. How many days and nights did Jesus fast in the wilderness?
A. Three   B. Seven   C. Twenty-one   D. Forty

680. What was Jesus' first temptation?
A. To bow before Satan   B. To jump from the temple
C. To turn stones into bread   D. To rule the world

681. What was Jesus' second temptation?
A. To rule the world   B. To turn stones into bread
C. To jump from the temple   D. To bow before Satan

682. What was Jesus' third temptation?
A. To turn stones into bread   B. To rule the world
C. To bow before Satan   D. To jump from the temple

683. How did Jesus resist these temptations?
A. The angels helped Him   B. He did not listen
C. He prayed to God   D. He quoted Scripture

684. How old was Jesus when He began His ministry?
A. Thirty   B. Twenty-five   C. Eighteen   D. Forty

685. Who said, "Behold the Lamb of God, which taketh away the sin of the world"?

A. John the Baptist   B. Jesus   C. Peter   D. Mary

686. Two of John's disciples followed Jesus. Name one of them.

A. Andrew   B. Peter   C. Judas   D. James

687. Who did Andrew first tell about Jesus?

A. Peter   B. James   C. Bartholomew   D. Philip

688. What does Cephas mean?

A. A stone   B. A king   C. A servant   D. A light

689. Who did Philip tell about Christ?

A. Nathaniel   B. John   C. Levi   D. Andrew

690. In what city was Jesus' first miracle?

A. Cana   B. Jerusalem   C. Bethlehem   D. Capernaum

691. What was Jesus' first miracle?

A. He turned water into wine   B. He healed blind Bartimaeus
C. He raised Lazarus from the dead   D. He healed ten lepers

692. Who came to see Jesus by night?

A. Nicodemus   B. Zacchaeus   C. John the Baptist   D. Caiaphas

693. In the Old Testament, who had "lifted up the serpent in the wilderness"?

A. Moses   B. God   C. Elijah   D. Aaron

694. In what country was Sychar?

A. Samaria   B. Galilee   C. Judea   D. Decapolis

695. How many husbands had the woman at the well had?

A. Five   B. One   C. Three   D. Seven

696. Jesus preached to the people from whose ship?

A. James'   B. John's   C. Thomas'   D. Peter's

697. What was Peter's other name?

A. Samuel   B. Simon   C. James   D. John

698. Who was Peter's brother?

A. Simon   B. James   C. John   D. Andrew

699. What did Peter and Andrew do for a living?

A. They were tax collectors   B. They were fishermen
C. They were soldiers   D. They were scribes

700. Jesus said, "I will make you _____ of men."

A. Respected   B. Harvesters   C. Loved   D. Fishers

701. Who was James' brother?
    A. Peter   B. John   C. Judas   D. Bartholomew

702. Who was James' and John's father?
    A. Simeon   B. Jochebed   C. Zebedee   D. Thomas

703. What was Levi's other name?
    A. Simon   B. Matthew   C. Mark   D. Jude

704. Who was Matthew's father?
    A. Jonas   B. Silas   C. Alphaeus   D. Cyrene

705. Who were called Boanerges?
    A. James and John   B. Peter and Andrew
    C. Jesus and John the Baptist   D. The twelve disciples

706. What does Boanerges mean?
    A. Sons of thunder   B. Sons of compassion
    C. Sons of Israel   D. Sons of heaven

707. Who was Didymus?
    A. Thomas   B. Levi   C. Jduas   D. James

708. Which disciple made a feast for Jesus?
    A. Peter   B. Matthew   C. Thomas   D. Judas

709. What was Matthew's occupation?
    A. Fisherman   B. Tax collector   C. Pharisee   D. Farmer

710. How many disciples did Jesus have?
    A. Twelve   B. Six   C. Fourteen   D. Twenty-Five

711. Which disciple's mother-in-law did Jesus heal?
    A. John's   B. Peter's   C. Thomas'   D. Philip's

712. In Jerusalem, Jesus healed a man by a pool which was called what?
    A. Bethesda   B. Siloam   C. Salem   D. Beautiful

713. How long had this lame man had his infirmity?
    A. Thirty-eight years   B. Ten years   C. Forty-seven years
    D. Fourteen years

714. Why did the Pharisees get mad when Jesus healed a man with a withered hand?
    A. They did not like the man
    B. Jesus had healed him on the Sabbath
    C. They did not get mad   D. They had wanted to heal the man

715. "This fellow doth not cast out devils, but by _____ the prince of the devils."
    A. Lucifer   B. Beelzebub   C. Satan   D. Baal

716. Jesus said the Pharisees would get the sign of the prophet
_____.

A. Isaiah   B. Jonah   C. Micah   D. Malachi

717. "Blessed are the poor in spirit: for _____."
A. They shall be comforted   B. They shall obtain mercy
C. Theirs is the kingdom of heaven   D. They shall see God

718. "Blessed are they that mourn: for _____."
A. They shall be called the children of God   B. They shall see God
C. They shall be filled   D. They shall be comforted

719. "Blessed are the meek: for _____."
A. Theirs is the kingdom of heaven
B. They shall obtain mercy   C. They shall see God
D. They shall inherit the earth

720. "Blessed are they which do hunger and thirst after righteousness: for
_____."
A. They shall be comforted   B. They shall see God
C. They shall obtain mercy   D. They shall be filled

721. "Blessed are the merciful: for _____."
A. They shall be called the children of God
B. They shall obtain mercy
C. Theirs is the kingdom of heaven
D. They shall inherit the earth

722. "Blessed are the pure in heart: for _____."
A. They shall be comforted   B. They shall be filled
C. They shall obtain mercy   D. They shall see God

723. "Blessed are the peacemakers: for _____."
A. They shall inherit the earth
B. They shall be called the children of God
C. They shall see God   D. They shall be comforted

724. "Blessed are they which are persecuted for righteousness' sake: for
_____."
A. They shall inherit the earth   B. They shall be filled
C. They shall obtain mercy   D. Theirs is the kingdom of heaven

725. "Blessed are ye when men shall revile you, and persecute you, and
shall say all manner of evil against you falsely for my sake.
_____."
A. Retaliate swiftly upon them
B. Rejoice, and be exceeding glad   C. Watch and pray
D. Vengeance is mine, saith the Lord

726. Jesus said Christians are the "salt of the earth" and the "_____ of the world."

A. Offscouring   B. Example   C. Light   D. Honorable

727. Jesus said, "_____ your enemies."

A. Respect   B. Hate   C. Love   D. Fight

728. "Behold the _____: for they sow not, neither do they reap."

A. Lilies of the field   B. Soldiers of Rome
C. Scribes and Pharisees   D. Fowls of the air

729. Jesus said Solomon was not arrayed like one of these. One of what?

A. The priests   B. Fowls of the air   C. Angels of God
D. Lilies of the field

730. Jesus said to seek what first?

A. Security   B. The kingdom of God
C. The friendship of the world   D. The joy of the Lord

731. Jesus said that whoever heard His words and did them was like a man who built his house on _____.

A. Sand   B. A rock   C. A mountain   D. Grass

732. Jesus said that whoever heard His words but did not do them was like a man who built his house on what?

A. A hill   B. Sand   C. A rock   D. Dreams

733. Who wanted Jesus just to speak a word so that his servant would be healed?

A. Peter   B. A centurion   C. Jairus   D. Martha

734. In what city did Jesus raise to life the only son of a widow woman?

A. Bethany   B. Jerusalem   C. Nain   D. Capernaum

735. What prisoner sent two disciples to see Jesus?

A. Barabbas   B. Peter   C. Judas   D. John the Baptist

736. John the Baptist condemned Herod for marrying _____.

A. Salome   B. Herodias   C. Drusilla   D. Bernice

737. Who had Herodias been married to?

A. Archelaus   B. Pilate   C. Philip   D. Caesar

738. Who danced before Herod?

A. John the Baptist   B. Herodias' daughter
C. Herodias   D. Pilate

739. Who had John the Baptist executed?

A. Jesus   B. Agrippa   C. Caesar   D. Herod

740. When Peter asked if he should forgive someone seven times, Jesus told him to forgive how many times?
A. 3   B. 12   C. 700   D. 70 times 7

741. Jesus said when an unclean spirit returns home he brings how many other spirits with him?
A. Two   B. Three   C. Five   D. Seven

742. Jesus said Jonah was a sign to _____.
A. The Israelites   B. Judah   C. The Syrians   D. The Ninevites

743. Jesus said that no man places a lighted candle
_____.
A. In a wind storm   B. In the daylight   C. Under a bushel
D. In the city

744. Jesus said five sparrows were sold for how many farthings?
A. Four   B. Three   C. Two   D. One

745. What was the rich fool going to do with his old barns?
A. Paint them   B. Tear them down   C. Move them   D. Sell them

746. Jesus likened Herod to what animal?
A. Owl   B. Fox   C. Donkey   D. Dove

747. Who "killest the prophets, and stonest them that are sent unto thee"?
A. Herod   B. Pilate   C. The Pharisees   D. Jerusalem

748. Who were James, Joses, Judas, and Simon?
A. Jesus' half brothers   B. Four of the disciples
C. Jewish priests   D. The Jewish high court

749. Who was called Legion?
A. The demoniac   B. The centurion
C. The twelve disciples   D. The family of God

750. Jesus allowed some demons to be cast into what animals?
A. Cows   B. Pigs   C. Sheep   D. Donkeys

751. The demons were cast into how many pigs?
A. 200   B. 2,000   C. 500   D. 5,000

752. Who was the ruler whose daughter was near death?
A. The centurion   B. Ananias   C. Jairus   D. Joel

753. What three disciples went with Jesus to Jairus' house?
A. Peter, Andrew, and James   B. Peter, James, and John
C. Andrew, Thomas, and Philip
D. Bartholomew, Judas, and Matthew

754. How old was Jairus' daughter?
A. Twelve   B. Six   C. Eighteen   D. Fourteen

755. Jesus healed a woman who had had a blood disease for how many years?
A. Twelve   B. Eighteen   C. Sixteen   D. Ten

756. Another name for the Sea of Galilee is the Sea of
_____.
A. Tiberias   B. Caesar   C. Capernaum   D. Salt

757. Whom did Jesus ask about feeding the multitude of people?
A. Philip   B. Peter   C. John   D. Thaddeus

758. Who told Jesus about the boy with a lunch?
A. Andrew   B. Philip   C. Matthew   D. Bartholomew

759. With how many loaves and fishes did Jesus feed the multitude?
A. One loaf and one fish   B. Five loaves and two fish
C. Ten loaves and five fish   D. Two loaves and five fish

760. How many people did Jesus feed?
A. 3,000   B. 5,000   C. 1,000   D. 1,500

761. How many baskets of food were left over?
A. Twelve   B. Seven   C. Five   D. Ten

762. Who walked on water?
A. Jesus   B. Andrew   C. James   D. John

763. Which disciple walked on water?
A. Bartholomew   B. Judas   C. John   D. Peter

764. Jesus used 7 loaves and a few fish to feed _____ people.
A. 5,000   B. 4,000   C. 3,000   D. 2,000

765. How many baskets of food were left over?
A. Twelve   B. Seven   C. Ten   D. Fourteen

766. Who sinned and caused the man to be born blind?
A. His father   B. The blind man   C. His parents   D. No one

767. Where did Jesus tell the blind man to go and wash?
A. The pool of Siloam   B. Jordan River
C. Dead Sea   D. Bethesda

768. Near what city did Jesus ask, "Whom do men say that I the Son of man am?"
A. Jerusalem   B. Caesarea Philippi   C. Nazareth   D. Sychar

769. Who did Peter say Jesus was?
A. A great teacher   B. The Christ
C. A great healer   D. The Deliver

770. What three disciples witnessed Jesus' transfiguration?
A. Peter, Andrew, and John   B. Peter, James, and John
C. James, Judas, and Philip   D. Peter, Andrew, and James

771. What two Old Testament characters appeared with Jesus?
A. Michael and Gabriel   B. Moses and Elijah
C. Elijah and Enoch   D. Noah and Abraham

772. What did Peter want to build for them?
A. Tabernacles   B. Towers   C. Altars   D. Images

773. From where did a voice say, "This is my beloved Son"?
A. From a cloud   B. From a whirlwind
C. From the fire   D. From an earthquake

774. What did Jesus say Peter would find in a fish's mouth?
A. A worm   B. A scroll   C. A hook   D. Money

775. Jesus said to become like whom in order to enter the kingdom of heaven?
A. Jesus   B. Children   C. Pharisees   D. God

776. Which disciples wanted to call fire from heaven to punish the Samaritans?
A. Peter and Andrew   B. Matthew and Thomas
C. Peter and Judas   D. James and John

777. How many people did Jesus send out by twos?
A. Thirty   B. Seventy   C. One hundred   D. Ten

778. When someone asked, "Who is my neighbor?", what parable did Jesus teach?
A. The Prodigal Son   B. The Good Samaritan
C. The Rich Fool   D. The Wheat and Tares

779. In the parable of the Good Samaritan, a man was robbed on his way to what city?
A. Jericho   B. Nazareth   C. Jerusalem   D. Bethany

780. Who was the first to pass the robbery victim?
A. A Samaritan   B. A Roman   C. A priest   D. A Levite

781. Who was the second to pass the robbery victim?
A. A Samaritan   B. A Roman   C. A priest   D. A Levite

782. Who was the third person to pass the robbery victim?
A. A Samaritan   B. A Roman   C. A priest   D. A Levite

783. Who was Martha's sister?
A. Miriam   B. Mary   C. Sarah   D. Elisabeth

784. Who was busy fixing dinner while Jesus taught?
    A. Mary B. Lazarus C. Peter D. Martha

785. The disciples said to Jesus, "Lord, teach us to pray, as _____ also taught his disciples."
    A. Eli B. Elisha C. Jeremiah D. John

786. Jesus said, "If a son shall ask bread of any of you that is a father, will he give him a _____ ?"
    A. Scorpion B. Snake C. Sneer D. Stone

787. A man had ninety-nine sheep at home, but how many were lost?
    A. Ten B. One C. One hundred D. twenty-three

788. A woman had ten pieces of silver and lost how many?
    A. Three B. One C. Ten D. Five

789. In the parable of the Prodigal Son, which son asked for his inheritance?
    A. The younger son B. The middle son
    C. The elder son D. All his sons

790. After he lost his money, what job did the Prodigal Son have?
    A. Feeding pigs B. Fishing
    C. A tax collector D. A soldier

791. When the Prodigal Son returned home, what did his father do?
    A. Made him a servant B. Sent him away
    C. Made him feed the pigs D. Threw a feast for him

792. Who refused to go to the feast?
    A. The younger son B. The elder son
    C. The father D. The servants

793. Who was the beggar who stayed at the rich man's gate?
    A. Bartimaeus B. Lazarus C. Simeon D. Titus

794. Where did Lazarus go when he died?
    A. Hell B. Abraham's bosom C. Utopia D. No where

795. Where did the rich man go when he died?
    A. Heaven B. Hell C. Abraham's bosom D. Utopia

796. What did the rich man want Lazarus to do?
    A. Bring him to heaven B. Nothing C. Visit him
    D. Give him a drop of water

797. How many brothers did the rich man have?
    A. Seven B. Five C. Three D. Zero

798. How many lepers did Jesus heal at one time?
    A. One B. Ten C. Zero D. Three

799. How many lepers returned to thank Jesus?
    A. One   B. Ten   C. Zero   D. Three

800. Of what nationality was the leper who thanked Jesus?
    A. Roman   B. Galilean   C. Judean   D. Samaritan

801. Jesus said to remember _____ wife.
    A. Peter's   B. Lot's   C. Abraham's   D. John's

802. From what town was Lazarus?
    A. Bethany   B. Jerusalem   D. Jericho   D. Bethlehem

803. Who were Lazarus' sisters?
    A. Mary and Martha   B. Salome and Joanna
    C. Mary and Salome   D. Martha and Joanna

804. How many days had Lazarus been dead?
    A. Four   B. One   C. Seven   D. Three

805. Who prevented the children from coming to Jesus?
    A. The disciples   B. Herod   C. Jesus   D. The Pharisees

806. What did Jesus do to the children?
    A. Rebuked them   B. Called them
    C. Disciplined them   D. Sent them away

807. After meeting Jesus, who went away sad because he had much riches?
    A. The rich young ruler   B. Nicodemus
    C. The prodigal son   D. Matthew

808. "It is easier for a _____ to go through the eye of a needle, than
    for a rich man to enter into the kingdom of God."
    A. Elephant   B. Rich man   D. Pharisee   D. Camel

809. Who was the blind man at Jericho that Jesus healed?
    A. Simon   B. Bartimaeus   C. Jairus   D. Cleopas

810. Where did Zacchaeus live?
    A. Jerusalem   B. Bethany   C. Jericho   D. Samaria

811. What was Zacchaeus' occupation?
    A. Tax collector   B. Centurion   C. Fisherman   D. Priest

812. What did Zacchaeus do in order to see Jesus?
    A. He climbed a tree   B. He looked down from a roof
    C. He stood on someone's shoulder   D. He sat on a camel

813. What kind of tree did he climb?
    A. Sycomore   B. Walnut   D. Oak   D. Olive

814. What did Jesus do to Zacchaeus?
    A. Rebuked him   B. Went to his house
    C. Made Zacchaeus leave town   D. Left him in the tree

815. Zacchaeus said he would repay how much?

A. Two-fold   B. Three-fold   C. Four-fold   D. Ten-fold

816. Who anointed the feet of Jesus?

A. Mary   B. Martha   C. Simon   D. Judas

817. Who said the ointment could have been sold?

A. Judas   B. Simon   C. Jesus   D. Martha

818. Jesus sent His disciples for a donkey while He was at

_____ .

A. Mount of Olives   B. Mt. Sinai
C. Mt. Zion   D. Mt. Moriah

819. What Old Testament prophet predicted Jesus would ride into Jerusalem on a donkey?

A. Isaiah   B. Jeremiah   C. Malachi   D. Zechariah

820. What kind of branches were placed before Jesus?

A. Palm   B. Sycamore   C. Cedar   D. Spruce

821. When the Pharisees rebuked the people for calling to Jesus, what did Jesus say would cry out?

A. Stones   B. Children   C. Palm trees   D. Priests

822. Who drove the moneychangers from the temple?

A. Caiaphas   B. Peter   C. The Pharisees   D. Jesus

823. "My house shall be called the house of prayer, but ye have made it a den of _____ ."

A. Iniquity   B. Lions   C. Thieves   D. Murderers

824. Why did Jesus curse the fig tree?

A. It was in the way   B. It was covered with leaves
C. It had no fruit   D. He didn't

825. "Render therefore unto Caesar the things which are Caesar's; and unto _____ the things that are God's."

A. Jesus   B. God   C. The temple   D. The priests

826. Jesus said the greatest commandment was to love _____ .

A. Yourself   B. Your neighbor   C. Others   D. God

827. Jesus said the second greatest commandment was to love

_____ .

A. God   B. Your neighbor   C. Jesus   D. Yourself

828. "But as the days of _____ were, so shall also the coming of the Son of Man be."

A. Isaiah   B. Noah   C. Abraham   D. Enoch

829. Jesus said Jerusalem would be trodden down by _____ .
   A. Romans   B. Jews   C. Gentiles   D. Samaritans

830. "Heaven and earth shall pass away: but my _____ shall not pass away."
   A. Disciples   B. Words   C. Example   D. Life

831. Which Jewish group did not believe in angels?
   A. Pharisees   B. Scribes   C. Sadducees   D. Zealots

832. Whom did Jesus commend for throwing two mites into the treasury?
   A. A widow   B. Judas   C. Nicodemus   D. Matthew

833. The woman who anointed Jesus with oil was in _____ house.
   A. Simon Peter's   B. Simon the leper's
   C. Mary and Martha's   D. John Mark's

834. How much could the ointment have been sold for?
   A. 30 pieces of silver   B. 500 pence
   C. 1 penny   D. 300 pence

835. What mother wanted her sons to sit by Jesus in His kingdom?
   A. Peter and Andrew's mother
   B. Philip and Bartholomew's mother
   C. Judas and Thomas' mother   D. James and John's mother

836. What two disciples were sent to prepare the passover?
   A. Peter and John   B. Peter and Andrew
   C. James and John   D. Thomas and Philip

837. Jesus told His disciples to follow a man carrying what?
   A. Bread   B. A pitcher   C. Palm leaves   D. Meat

838. Where was the passover held?
   A. In the temple   B. In the upper room
   C. At Peter's house   D. In Bethlehem

839. Who did not want their feet washed?
   A. Peter   B. Judas   C. James   D. Andrew

840. Who wanted to sift Simon as wheat?
   A. Satan   B. Jesus   C. Pilate   D. Judas

841. How many swords did the disciples have?
   A. Zero   B. One   C. Two   D. Three

842. In what garden did Jesus pray?
   A. The flower garden   B. The Garden of Eden
   C. The Olivet garden   D. The Garden of Gethsemane

843. What three disciples did Jesus ask to pray with Him?
    A. Peter, James, and John   B. Matthew, Mark, and Luke
    C. Philip, Thomas, and Jude   D. John, James, and Judas

844. How many times did Jesus catch the disciples sleeping?
    A. One   B. Five   C. Zero   D. Three

845. Who betrayed Jesus?
    A. Peter   B. Judas   C. Thomas   D. Philip

846. How many pieces of silver did Judas receive for betraying Jesus?
    A. Thirty   B. Twenty   C. One hundred   D. Forty

847. With what sign did Judas betray Jesus?
    A. He pointed at Jesus   B. He kissed Jesus
    C. He swung a sword at Jesus   D. He hugged Jesus

848. Which disciple cut off the servant's ear?
    A. Peter   B. John   C. Philip   D. James

849. What was the name of the servant whose ear was cut off?
    A. Malchus   B. Simeon   C. Annas   D. Caiaphas

850. What was the highpriest's name?
    A. Pilate   B. Justus   C. Ananias   D. Caiaphas

851. Who was Caiaphas' father-in-law?
    A. Annas   B. Pilate   C. Herod   D. Caesar

852. How did Judas die?
    A. The priests killed him   B. He hanged himself
    C. He was struck by lightning   D. The disciples killed him

853. What was purchased with the money Judas threw on the temple floor?
    A. New garments for the priests   B. The potter's field
    C. A new altar   D. A tomb for Jesus

854. Who was governor over Judea?
    A. Herod   B. Pilate   C. Caiaphas   D. Caesar

855. To whom did Pilate send Jesus?
    A. Herod   B. Caesar   C. No one   D. Judas

856. Pilate sent Jesus to Herod because Jesus was from where?
    A. Samaria   B. Judea   C. Pontus   D. Galilee

857. What did Jesus tell Herod?
    A. That he was evil   B. Nothing
    C. That he was an adulterer   D. That He was innocent

858. Who said, "What is truth?"
    A. Pilate   B. Herod   C. Jesus   D. Caiaphas

859. What prisoner did Pilate release?
A. Jesus   B. Judas   C. Herod   D. Barabbas

860. Who had a dream about Jesus and warned Pilate?
A. Herod   B. Pilate's wife   C. Caiaphas   D. Peter

861. The crowd said that Pilate would not be whose friend if he released Jesus?
A. Caesar's   B. Herod's   C. The Jews'   D. The Priests'

862. What was placed on Jesus' head?
A. A golden crown   B. A crown of thorns
C. A scarlet hood   D. A laurel wreath

863. Who carried Jesus' cross?
A. Simon of Cyrene   B. Peter   C. Judas   D. Barabbas

864. Who was Alexander and Rufus' father?
A. Judas   B. Simon of Cyrene   C. Matthew   D. Nicodemus

865. Who did Jesus tell to "weep for yourselves"?
A. The disciples   B. Peter and Judas   C. The priests
D. The women of Jerusalem

866. Where was Jesus crucified?
A. Bethany   B. Calvary   C. Rome   D. Capernaum

867. The word Golgotha comes from what language?
A. Hebrew   B. Greek   C. Latin   D. Egyptian

868. What does Golgotha mean?
A. The hill of remorse   B. The hill of executions
C. God's accursed   D. The place of a skull

869. How many others were crucified with Jesus?
A. Two   B. Zero   C. Three   D. Five

870. Who cast lots for Jesus' robe?
A. The disciples   B. The priests
C. The Sanhedrin   D. The soldiers

871. What inscription was on Jesus' cross?
A. The King of Kings   B. The King of the Jews
C. The King of Israel   D. The King of Despair

872. In what three languages was the inscription?
A. Greek, Latin, and Egyptian
B. Latin, Hebrew, and Greek
C. Hebrew, Greek, and Syrian
D. Assyrian, Latin, and Egyptian

873. To whom did Jesus say, "Today thou shalt be with me in paradise"?
A. Pilate   B. The centurion   C. The thief   D. Peter

874. At Jesus' crucifixion, what was ripped in the temple?
A. The altar   B. The laver   C. The veil   D. The ark

875. Who said, "Truly this man was the Son of God"?
A. Nicodemus   B. Joseph of Arimathea
C. The centurion   D. Pilate

876. What did the soldiers do to the ones being crucified?
A. Broke their legs   B. Speared them
C. Watched them   D. Left them

877. What did they do to Jesus?
A. Pierced His side   B. Nothing
C. Buried Him   D. Broke His legs

878. Who asked for Jesus' body?
A. Peter   B. Mary   C. John   D. Joseph of Arimathaea

879. With whom did Pilate check to confirm Jesus' death?
A. Herod   B. No one   C. Joseph of Arimathea
D. The centurion

880. Who helped Joseph of Arimathea bury Jesus?
A. Nicodemus   B. Peter   C. Judas   D. James

881. On which day was Jesus resurrected?
A. Friday   B. Sunday   C. Saturday   D. Thursday

882. Who frightened the women who came to the tomb?
A. The guards   B. The disciples.   C. Pilate   D. An angel

883. To whom did Jesus first appear after His resurrection?
A. The women   B. Mary Magdalene   C. Peter   D. John

884. How many demons had been cast out of Mary Magdalene?
A. Twelve   B. Seven   C. Twenty-one   D. Fourteen

885. Which two disciples ran to the sepulcher?
A. Peter and John   B. Philip and Andrew   C. James and John
D. Thomas and Matthew

886. Who said that the disciples had stolen Jesus' body?
A. The guards   B. The disciples   C. Pilate   D. Herod

887. To what village were two of the disciples walking?
A. Jerusalem   B. Bethany   C. Emmaus   D. Samaria

888. These two recognized Jesus when Jesus did what?
A. Told them His name   B. Broke bread   C. Disappeared
D. Spoke to them

889. To what city did the two return?
   A. Bethlehem   B. Jerusalem   C. Nazareth   D. Emmaus

890. Which disciple doubted that Jesus was alive?
   A. Thomas   B. John   C. Peter   D. Andrew

891. To whom did Jesus say, "Lovest thou me more than these?"
   A. Peter   B. James   C. John   D. Thomas

892. To whom is the Book of Acts addressed?
   A. The church at Jerusalem   B. The apostles
   C. Theophilus   D. All Christians

893. How many days was Christ seen after His resurrection?
   A. Forty   B. Twenty   C. Fifty   D. Thirty

894. In what city did Jesus tell the disciples to wait?
   A. Bethlehem   B. Jerusalem   C. Nazareth   D. Capernaum

895. From what mount did Jesus ascend into heaven?
   A. Mt. Sinai   B. Mt. Horeb   C. Mt. Moriah   D. Mt. of Olives

896. How many were together in the upper room?
   A. Eleven   B. Five hundred   C. One hundred twenty   D. Twenty

897. Who was selected to take Judas' place?
   A. Matthias   B. Mark   C. Luke   D. Paul

898. On what Jewish holiday were the disciples filled with the Holy Ghost?
   A. Passover   B. Purim   C. Pentecost   D. Day of Atonement

899. Why were the people astonished at the disciples?
   A. The people heard the disciples speak their own language
   B. The disciples were drunk   C. The people heard a rushing wind
   D. The people saw flames of fire on the disciples' heads

900. What did the people think about the disciples?
   A. That they were God's ministers   B. That they were frauds
   C. That they were lying   D. That they were drunk

901. Who preached to the people on the day of Pentecost?
   A. Paul   B. John   C. Peter   D. James

902. What Old Testament prophet did Peter quote?
   A. Joel   B. Isaiah   C. Jeremiah   D. Elijah

903. Peter said the young men would have visions and the old men would
   _____.
   A. Also have visions   B. Dream dreams   C. Hear voices
   D. Inspire others

904. How many people were added to the church on the day of Pentecost?

A. 120   B. 7,000   C. 33   D. 3,000

905. What two disciples went up to the temple to pray?

A. Peter and John   B. James and John
C. Peter and Andrew   D. Matthew and Philip

906. At the temple, a lame man sat at the gate called _____.

A. Eastern   B. Siloam   C. Beautiful   D. Bethesda

907. How old was the lame man who Peter healed?

A. Forty   B. Twenty   C. Sixty   D. Thirty

908. When the council questioned the disciples, who answered the council?

A. Thomas   B. Peter   C. James   D. John

909. What was Barnabas' country?

A. Cyprus   B. Judea   C. Crete   D. Cilicia

910. What couple lied to the Holy Ghost and died?

A. Aquila and Priscilla   B. Felix and Drusilla
C. Lois and Eunice   D. Ananias and Sapphira

911. Who gave advice to the council concerning the disciples?

A. Annas   B. Gamaliel   C. Caiaphas   D. Nicodemus

912. How many deacons were chosen to help the disciples?

A. Seven   B. Twelve   C. Five   D. Ten

913. Who was stoned to death?

A. Peter   B. Philip   C. Stephen   D. Mark

914. Who was the chief persecutor of the church?

A. Saul   B. Silas   C. Thomas   D. Barnabas

915. Who preached to the people of Samaria?

A. Paul   B. James   C. Philip   D. Thomas

916. What two disciples were sent to Samaria?

A. James and John   B. Paul and Silas
C. Andrew and Levi   D. Peter and John

917. Who told Philip to go to the desert?

A. An angel   B. Peter   C. Jesus   D. God

918. Whom did Philip meet in the desert?

A. A Samaritan   B. An eunuch   C. A Roman soldier   D. A priest

919. Who was queen of the Ethiopians?

A. Esther   B. Candace   C. Vashti   D. Sheba

920. What Old Testament book was the eunuch reading?
A. Isaiah   B. Jeremiah   C. Psalms   D. Daniel

921. To what city was Saul headed when he was struck down by a light?
A. Tyre   B. Rome   C. Jerusalem   D. Damascus

922. After he saw the light, what was physically wrong with Saul?
A. He was blind   B. He was deaf   C. He was dumb   D. He was lame

923. In Damascus, in whose house did Saul stay?
A. Saul's   B. Ananias'   C. Judas'   D. Philip's

924. The house Saul stayed in was on a street called what?
A. Beautiful   B. Straight   C. Main   D. Narrow

925. Who touched Saul and restored his sight?
A. Barnabas   B. Silas   C. Judas   D. Ananias

926. How did Saul escape from Damascus?
A. He was let down over a wall in a basket.
B. He hid in a cart of straw   C. He hid in a huge stone jar
D. He disguised himself as a priest

927. When the disciples didn't trust Saul at Jerusalem, who vouched for him?
A. Barnabas   B. Peter   C. James   D. Silas

928. Who did Peter heal of the palsy?
A. Agabus   B. Aeneas   C. Aquilla   D. Agrippa

929. How long had he been sick with the palsy?
A. Eight years   B. Eighteen years   C. Twenty-eight years
D. Thirty-eight years

930. Who had died at Joppa?
A. James   B. Philip   C. Thomas   D. Tabitha

931. What was her other name?
A. Lydia   B. Eunice   C. Dorcas   D. Euodia

932. Who raised her from the dead?
A. Peter   B. James   C. Jesus   D. Paul

933. In whose house did Peter stay at Joppa?
A. Saul's   B. Mark's   C. Philip's   D. Simon's

934. In what city did Cornelius live?
A. Joppa   B. Caesarea   C. Jerusalem   D. Capernaum

935. Who saw a vision of a sheet descending from heaven with animals on it?
A. Cornelius   B. Saul   C. Simon   D. Peter

936. In what city were Jesus' followers first called Christians?
A. Antioch   B. Jerusalem   C. Rome   D. Caesarea

937. Who had James killed?
A. Caesar   B. Herod   C. Felix   D. Festus

938. After James' death, which disciple was arrested?
A. John   B. Thomas   C. Peter   D. Bartholomew

939. Who led Peter from the prison?
A. An angel   B. John   C. Saul   D. Barnabas

940. To whose house did Peter go?
A. Philip's   B. Peter's   C. John's   D. Mary's

941. Whose mother was she?
A. Peter's   B. Luke's   C. Mark's   D. Silas'

942. Who forgot to open the door and let Peter in?
A. Mary   B. Mark   C. Rhoda   D. Barnabas

943. Which ruler was killed because he didn't give glory to God?
A. Caesar   B. Felix   C. Festus   D. Herod

944. Who was the deputy of Cyprus?
A. Simon Magus   B. Sergius Paulus   C. Elymas   D. Ananias

945. What was Saul's other name?
A. Silas   B. Paul   C. Barnabas   D. Mark

946. Who left Paul and Barnabas at Perga?
A. Silas   B. John Mark   C. Titus   D. Timothy

947. After a man was healed, what did the people call Barnabas?
A. Jupiter   B. Mercury   C. Apollo   D. Pluto

948. After a man was healed, what did the people call Paul?
A. Mercury   B. Neptune   C. Jupiter   D. Apollo

949. Who was stoned at Lystra?
A. Barnabas   B. Mark   C. Silas   D. Paul

950. Whom did Paul and Barnabas argue over?
A. Silas   B. Timothy   C. John Mark   D. Titus

951. Who went with Barnabas?
A. John Mark   B. Paul   C. Silas   D. Peter

952. Who went with Paul?
A. John Mark   B. Barnabas   C. Silas   D. Peter

953. Whom did Paul and Silas take with them at Lystra?
A. Peter   B. Titus   C. Luke   D. Timothy

954. The Holy Spirit prevented Paul from preaching where?
A. Asia   B. Rome   C. Jerusalem   D. Caesarea

955. In what city did Paul have a vision?
A. Jerusalem   B. Ephesus   C. Antioch   D. Troas

956. In his vision Paul saw a man of _____.
A. Rome   B. Macedonia   C. Crete   D. Cyprus

957. Who was the seller of purple at Philippi?
A. Lydia   B. Tabitha   C. Priscilla   D. Dorcas

958. Where did Paul and Silas sing hymns at midnight?
A. In prison   B. At Lydia's house   C. By the river
D. In the synagogue

959. Who said, "What must I do to be saved?"
A. Lydia   B. A prisoner   C. The jailer   D. Silas

960. In what city did the people proclaim, "They that have turned the
world upside down have come to us also"?
A. Philippi   B. Ephesus   C. Thessalonica   D. Rome

961. In what city were Paul and Silas received with readiness?
A. Thessalonica   B. Berea   C. Ephesus   D. Corinth

962. To what city did Paul go after Berea?
A. Corinth   B. Ephesus   C. Rome   D. Athens

963. Who preached on Mars' Hill?
A. Peter   B. Paul   C. Apollos   D. Silas

964. Who was Aquila's wife?
A. Lydia   B. Priscilla   C. Lois   D. Eunice

965. What was Aquila's and Priscilla's occupation?
A. Tentmakers   B. Weavers   C. Merchants   D. Potters

966. At Ephesus the people burned their magic books which were worth
how many pieces of silver?
A. 500   B. 1,500   C. 5,000   D. 50,000

967. Who was the silversmith who caused trouble for Paul?
A. Damaris   B. Apollos   C. Demetrius   D. Claudius

968. He made shrines for which goddess?
A. Diana   B. Aphrodite   C. Isis   D. Venus

969. Who fell from a window while Paul was preaching?
A. Eutychus   B. Mark   C. Dorcas   D. Lydia

970. On his way to Jerusalem, Paul gave a farewell address to
_____ elders.
A. Antioch's   B. Ephesus'   C. Corinth's   D. Philippi's

971. Whom did Paul stay with at Caesarea?
A. John   B. Barnabas   C. Peter   D. Philip

972. Philip was one of the seven _____.
A. Bishops   B. Elders   C. Deacons   D. Disciples

973. How many daughters did Philip have?
A. Two   B. Four   C. Eight   D. Ten

974. Where was Paul accused of defiling the temple?
A. In the temple   B. In the synagogue
C. In the Sanhedrin   D. In Peter's house

975. The chief captain thought Paul was of what nationalty?
A. Roman   B. Ethiopian   C. Greek   D. Egyptian

976. From what city was Paul?
A. Tarsus   B. Damascus   C. Samaria   D. Antioch

977. From which of the Jewish tribes was Paul?
A. Dan   B. Benjamin   C. Levi   D. Judah

978. Who was Paul's Jewish teacher?
A. Apollos   B. Jesus   C. Silas   D. Gamaliel

979. A riot broke out when Paul mentioned what word?
A. Jesus   B. Passover   C. Gentiles   D. Romans

980. What prevented the Romans from whipping Paul?
A. Paul was a Roman citizen   B. Paul was a Jewish citizen
C. Paul gave them money   D. Paul was innocent

981. How many people had formed a conspiracy to kill Paul?
A. Ten   B. Twenty   C. Thirty   D. Forty

982. Who told Paul of the conspiracy?
A. His uncle   B. His brother   C. His nephew   D. His sister

983. Paul was taken from Jerusalem to _____.
A. Rome   B. Caesarea   C. Antioch   D. Ephesus

984. Who was the governor Paul appeared before?
A. Felix   B. Pilate   C. Herod   D. Agrippa

985. Who was Felix's wife?
A. Bernice   B. Priscilla   C. Lydia   D. Drusilla

986. Who succeeded Felix?
A. Agrippa   B. Herod   C. Festus   D. Claudius

987. To whom did Paul appeal?
A. Caesar   B. Herod   C. The Sanhedrin   D. God

988. What king came to visit Festus?
A. Caesar   B. Felix   C. Agrippa   D. Nero

989. Who accompanied the king?
A. Bernice   B. Drusilla   C. Diana   D. Mary

990. Who said, "Almost thou persuadest me to be a Christian"?
A. Festus   B. Paul   C. Bernice   D. Agrippa

991. What was called Euroclydon?
A. The ship   B. The wind   C. The port   D. The crew

992. On which island was Paul stranded?
A. Melita   B. Crete   C. Cyprus   D. Sicily

993. Who was bitten by a poisonous snake but did not die?
A. The centurion   B. Silas   C. Luke   D. Paul

994. In what city was Paul imprisoned?
A. Rome   B. Corinth   C. Ephesus   D. Antioch

995. Who was Timothy's grandmother?
A. Mary   B. Lydia   C. Lois   D. Eunice

996. Who was Timothy's mother?
A. Martha   B. Lois   C. Eunice   D. Drusilla

997. Who is the archangel?
A. Gabriel   B. Apollyon   C. Michael   D. Justus

998. Who wrote the Book of Revelation?
A. Paul   B. John   C. Peter   D. Jude

999. To how many churches of Asia did John write?
A. Three   B. Seven   C. Twelve   D. Forty

1000. On what island was John when he wrote the Book of Revelation?
A. Patmos   B. Melita   C. Crete   D. Cyprus

1001. Where will the earth's last battle be fought?
A. Rome   B. Cilicia   C. Egypt   D. Armageddon

Answers and References

1. B. Gen. 1:1
2. D. Gen. 1:3-5
3. B. Gen. 2:2
4. D. Gen. 2:7
5. B. Gen. 2:22
6. C. Gen. 3:20
7. C. Gen. 3:20
8. D. Gen. 3:20
9. D. Gen. 2:8
10. B. Gen. 3:1-5
11. B. Gen. 2:17 & Gen. 3:6
12. B. Gen. 3:21
13. D. Gen. 3:24
14. B. Gen. 4:1-2
15. B. Gen. 4:8
16. A. Gen. 4:9
17. A. Gen. 4:25
18. D. Gen. 5:24
19. B. Gen. 5:27
20. D. Gen. 5:27
21. B. Gen. 6:13-14
22. D. Gen. 5:32
23. B. Gen. 7:13
24. D. Gen. 7:4
25. B. Gen. 8:4
26. C. Gen. 8:7
27. C. Gen. 8:8
28. D. Gen. 8:8,10,12
29. D. Gen. 9:13
30. D. Gen. 11:9
31. D. Gen. 12:5
32. B. Gen. 12:5
33. B. Gen. 13:8
34. B. Gen. 16:1
35. D. Gen. 16:15
36. A. Gen. 19:16
37. A. Gen. 19:26
38. B. Gen. 21:3
39. B. Gen. 21:6
40. D. Gen. 21:5
41. B. Gen. 17:17 & Gen. 21:5
42. D. Gen. 21:9
43. B. Gen. 22:2
44. D. Gen. 22:11
45. B. Gen. 22:13
46. C. Gen. 23:1
47. C. Gen. 24:67
48. D. Gen. 25:7
49. D. Gen. 25:25-26
50. B. Gen. 25:28
51. B. Gen. 25:28
52. B. Gen. 27:19
53. D. Gen. 28:11
54. B. Gen. 28:12
55. B. Gen. 29:18
56. A. Gen. 29:20
57. A. Gen. 29:16
58. B. Gen. 27:42-43
59. D. Gen. 29:25
60. C. Gen. 29:30
61. A. Gen. 32:24
62. D. Gen. 32:28
63. A. Gen. 34:1 & Gen. 35:22
64. C. Gen. 35:8
65. A. Gen. 36:8
66. C. Gen. 37:3
67. D. Gen. 37:3
68. C. Gen. 37:22
69. D. Gen. 37:28
70. C. Gen. 37:28
71. A. Gen. 37:31
72. C. Gen. 37:32
73. A. Gen. 37:36
74. D. Gen. 39:17-20
75. A. Gen. 40:5-8
76. D. Gen. 40:22
77. C. Gen. 41:2-7
78. C. Gen. 41:9-12
79. C. Gen. 41:26-30
80. D. Gen. 41:33-36
81. B. Gen. 41:39-40
82. D. Gen. 41:46
83. B. Gen. 41-29
84. D. Gen. 41:30
85. B. Gen. 41:51-52
86. C. Gen. 42:1-2
87. C. Gen. 42:4
88. D. Gen. 42:8-9
89. D. Gen. 42:24
90. D. Gen. 42:15-16
91. B. Gen. 43:2
92. D. Gen. 43:15
93. B. Gen. 44:2
94. D. Gen. 45:3
95. B. Gen. 47:1
96. C. Gen. 46:34
97. C. Gen. 47:28
98. D. Gen. 48:14
99. D. Gen. 50:26
100. B. Gen. 50:24-25
101. B. Exod. 1:10
102. B. Exod. 1:16
103. D. Exod. 1:19
104. B. Exod. 1:22
105. B. Exod. 2:1
106. A. Exod. 6:20
107. A. Exod. 2:2
108. D. Exod. 2:3
109. B. Exod. 2:4
110. B. Exod. 15:20
111. B. Exod. 2:5
112. B. Exod. 2:7-8
113. D. Exod. 2:10
114. B. Exod. 2:11-12
115. B. Exod. 2:13
116. A. Exod. 2:14
117. A. Exod. 2:15
118. D. Exod. 2:21
119. B. Exod. 2:18
120. B. Exod. 2:22
121. B. Exod. 3:1
122. B. Exod. 3:2
123. D. Exod. 3:1
124. B. Exod. 3:10
125. B. Exod. 3:8
126. D. Exod. 4:14
127. D. Exod. 4:27
128. D. Exod. 5:2
129. D. Exod. 7:7
130. C. Exod. 7:11-12
131. C. Exod. 7:12

132. B. Exod. 7:20
133. D. Exod. 8:6
134. B. Exod. 8:17
135. B. Exod. 8:24
136. B. Exod. 7:21-22 &
    Exod. 8:7
137. D. Exod. 8:22
138. B. Exod. 9:3
139. B. Exod. 9:10
140. A. Exod. 9:23
141. A. Exod. 10:13
142. D. Exod. 10:22
143. B. Exod. 12:11
144. B. Exod. 12:22
145. B. Exod. 12:29
146. B. Exod. 12:29
147. D. Exod. 13:4
148. B. Exod. 12:41
149. B. Exod. 13:19
150. A. Exod. 13:21
151. A. Exod. 13:21
152. D. Exod. 14:15-16
153. B. Exod. 15:20
154. B. Exod. 16:15
155. C. Exod. 16:20
156. A. Exod. 16:27
157. A. Exod. 16:33
158. A. Exod. 17:6
159. B. Exod. 17:9
160. C. Exod. 17:11
161. B. Exod. 17:12
162. A. Exod. 18:4
163. A. Exod. 18:21-22
164. A. Exod. 19:20
165. C. Exod. 20:3
166. B. Exod. 20:4
167. A. Exod. 20:7
168. B. Exod. 20:8
169. A. Exod. 20:12
170. C. Exod. 20:13
171. A. Exod. 20:14
172. D. Exod. 20:15
173. B. Exod. 20:16
174. D. Exod. 20:17
175. B. Exod. 24:18
176. B. Exod. 25:20
177. C. Exod. 28:4
178. C. Exod. 28:1

179. D. Exod. 31:18
180. B. Exod. 32:3-4
181. B. Exod. 32:10
182. B. Exod. 32:11-12
183. D. Exod. 32:17
184. B. Exod. 32:19
185. B. Exod. 32:20
186. A. Exod. 33:23
187. A. Exod. 34:29
188. D. Exod. 34:33
189. B. Exod. 40:37
190. D. Exod. 40:36
191. B. Num. 1:3
192. D. Num. 1:49
193. C. Num. 1:50
194. D. Num. 2:3,5,7,10,
    12,14,18,20,22,
    25,27,29
195. B. Num. 3:4
196. C. Num. 9:16
197. C. Num. 9:16
198. B. Num. 11:31
199. B. Num. 12:1
200. D. Num. 12:10
201. B. Num. 12:13
202. B. Num. 12:14
203. A. Num. 13:2
204. A. Num. 13:23
205. D. Num. 13:25
206. B. Num. 13:33
207. D. Num. 14:6-9
208. B. Num. 14:6-7
209. D. Num. 14:12
210. B. Num. 14:13
211. D. Num. 14:29-30
212. B. Num. 14:30
213. C. Num. 14:33
214. C. Num. 14:34
215. D. Num. 14:37
216. D. Num. 16:1-2
217. B. Num. 16:31-32
218. A. Num. 17:3
219. A. Num. 17:8
220. B. Heb. 9:4
221. B. Num. 20:1
222. D. Num. 20:8
223. B. Num. 20:11
224. D. Num. 20:12

225. D. Num. 20:25-28
226. B. Num. 20:28
227. D. Num. 21:6
228. D. Num. 21:8
229. B. Num. 21:8
230. D. Num. 22:4-6
231. B. Num. 22:4
232. B. Num. 22:27
233. A. Num. 22:28
234. A. Num. 22:31
235. D. Num. 24:10
236. A. Num. 27:18
237. C. Num. 31:8
238. A. Num. 33:39
239. D. Deut. 11:29
240. C. Deut. 11:29
241. D. Deut. 17:16-17
242. C. Deut. 34:1
243. A. Deut. 34:5
244. D. Deut. 34:5-6
245. A. Deut. 34:7
246. C. Josh. 1:1
247. D. Josh. 2:1
248. B. Josh. 2:1
249. D. Josh. 2:13
250. B. Josh. 2:15
251. C. Josh. 2:18
252. C. Josh. 2:18
253. D. Josh. 3:15-16
254. D. Josh. 4:3
255. B. Josh. 4:9
256. D. Josh. 4:20
257. D. Josh. 5:10
258. B. Josh. 5:12
259. C. Josh. 6:4
260. D. Josh. 6:11
261. D. Josh. 6:14
262. D. Josh. 6:15
263. B. Josh. 6:16
264. D. Josh. 6:20
265. B. Josh. 6:23
266. D. Josh. 8:26
267. B. Josh. 9:3-6
268. D. Josh. 10:11
269. D. Josh. 10:13
270. D. Josh. 10:13
271. C. Josh. 22:1,4
272. B. Josh. 13:33

273. B. Josh. 22:32
274. D. Josh. 24:2,15
275. A. Josh. 24:29
276. A. Josh. 24:32
277. A. Judg. 4:4
278. A. Judg. 4:6
279. B. Judg. 4:8
280. D. Judg. 4:18,21
281. B. Judg. 6:11
282. B. Judg. 6:37-38
283. B. Judg. 6:39
284. D. Judg. 7:7
285. C. Judg. 7:16
286. A. Judg. 11:1-2
287. B. Judg. 11:9:11
288. A. Judg. 11:30-31
289. B. Judg. 11:34
290. C. Judg. 12:6
291. B. Judg. 13:22,24
292. C. Judg. 13:3
293. B. Judg. 13:20
294. A. Judg. 14:5-6
295. A. Judg. 14:8
296. A. Judg. 14:15-17
297. D. Judg. 15:4-5
298. D. Judg. 15:15
299. C. Judg. 16:3
300. B. Judg. 16:4
301. B. Judg. 16:6-7
302. D. Judg. 16:11
303. A. Judg. 16:13
304. A. Judg. 16:17
305. B. Judg. 16:19
306. B. Judg. 16:27
307. D. Ruth 1:2
308. D. Ruth 1:1
309. B. Ruth 1:2
310. B. Ruth 1:2
311. B. Ruth 1:4
312. D. Ruth 1:16
313. A. Ruth 1:20
314. A. Ruth 2:3
315. B. Ruth 4:13
316. B. Ruth 4:21
317. D. Ruth 4:21-22
318. B. I Sam. 1:1-2
319. B. I Sam. 1:11
320. D. I Sam. 1:12

321. B. I Sam. 1:13
322. C. I Sam. 1:20
323. D. I Sam. 2:19
324. D. I Sam. 2:34
325. B. I Sam. 2:22-23
326. B. I Sam. 2:34
327. B. I Sam. 3:4
328. D. I Sam. 3:5,6,8
329. B. I Sam. 3:14
330. B. I Sam. 4:3
331. A. I Sam. 4:11
332. A. I Sam. 4:18
333. D. I Sam. 6:1
334. B. I Sam. 8:5
335. D. I Sam. 9:1-2
336. A. I Sam. 9:21
337. A. I Sam. 9:3
338. B. I Sam. 9:9
339. D. I Sam. 10:22
340. B. I Sam. 13:16
341. C. I Sam. 14:50
342. D. I Sam. 16:1
343. B. I Sam. 16:13
344. B. I Sam. 16:23
345. B. I Sam. 17:4
346. D. I Sam. 17:49
347. B. I Sam. 18:7
348. B. I Sam. 18:11
349. A. I Sam. 18:1
350. A. I Sam. 18:27
351. D. I Sam. 19:10
352. B. I Sam. 19:12
353. A. I Sam. 22:18
354. C. I Sam. 22:20-21
355. A. I Sam. 23:16-18
356. C. I Sam. 24:4
357. D. I Sam. 24:9-11
358. C. I Sam. 25:1
359. D. I Sam. 25:3
360. C. I Sam. 25:3
361. A. I Sam. 25:18
362. C. I Sam. 25:38
363. A. I Sam. 25:42
364. A. I Sam. 26:7
365. D. I Sam. 26:8
366. C. I Sam. 26:12
367. C. I Sam. 26:14
368. B. I Sam. 28:7

369. D. I Sam. 28:11
370. D. I Sam. 28:17
371. B. I Sam. 28:19
372. B. I Sam. 31:1-2
373. C. I Sam. 31:4
374. C. I Sam. 31:5
375. D. I Sam. 31:10
376. D. I Sam. 31:11-12
377. B. I Sam. 31:13
378. B. II Sam. 2:4
379. D. II Sam. 2:13
380. B. II Sam. 5:4
381. D. II Sam. 5:4
382. B. II Sam. 5:11
383. D. II Sam. 6:16
384. D. II Sam. 6:16
385. D. II Sam. 7:5
386. D. II Sam. 7:17
387. C. I Chron. 28:3
388. B. II Sam. 11:2-3
389. D. II Sam. 11:3
390. B. II Sam. 11:6
391. B. II Sam. 11:9
392. A. II Sam. 11:13
393. A. II Sam. 11:15
394. D. II Sam. 11:26-27
395. B. II Sam. 12:1
396. B. II Sam. 12:7
397. B. II Sam. 12:14
398. B. II Sam. 12:24
399. D. II Sam. 12:25
400. A. II Sam. 15:10
401. A. II Sam. 15:12
402. C. II Sam. 15:37
403. A. II Sam. 16:5-6
404. A. II Sam. 16:11
405. B. II Sam. 17:1
406. C. II Sam. 17:14
407. A. II Sam. 17:23
408. C. II Sam. 18:5
409. B. II Sam. 18:9
410. A. II Sam. 18:14
411. A. II Sam. 19:16
412. D. II Sam. 19:39
413. B. II Sam. 20:1
414. D. II Sam. 20:10
415. B. II Sam. 20:15,22
416. C. II Sam. 21:19

417. D. II Sam. 21:20
418. B. II Sam. 24:1
419. B. II Sam. 24:2
420. D. II Sam. 24:11
421. B. II Sam. 24:13
422. B. II Sam. 24-13
423. A. II Sam. 24:13
424. A. II Sam. 24:15
425. D. II Sam. 24:16
426. B. II Sam. 24:25
427. C. II Sam. 24:22-23
428. A. I Kings 1:3
429. D. I Kings 1:5
430. C. I Kings 1:34
431. A. I Kings 2:17
432. C. I Kings 2:24-25
433. D. I Kings 2:26
434. C. I Kings 2:33-34
435. D. I Kings 2:36
436. A. I Kings 2:44-46
437. A. I Kings 3:1
438. B. I Kings 3:9
439. C. I Kings 3:13-14
440. A. I Kings 3:25
441. A. I Kings 3:26-27
442. A. I Kings 4:32
443. B. I Kings 4:32
444. C. I Kings 5:1
445. B. I Kings 5:6
446. D. I Kings 5:6
447. D. I Kings 5:11
448. B. I Kings 6:1
449. A. II Chron. 7:1
450. D. I Kings 7:1
451. B. I Kings 10:1
452. C. I Kings 12:1
453. C. I Kings 12:20
454. D. I Kings 12:28
455. C. I Kings 12:29
456. A. I Kings 16:23-24
457. A. I Kings 16:34
458. C. I Kings 16:30-31
459. A. I Kings 17:1
460. A. I Kings 17:6
461. B. I Kings 17:10
462. C. I Kings 17:14
463. B. I Kings 17:20-22
464. D. I Kings 18:19

465. A. I Kings 18:22
466. C. I Kings 18:36-38
467. A. I Kings 18:40
468. C. I Kings 18:42-44
469. D. I Kings 19:2
470. C. I Kings 19:4
471. D. I Kings 19:8
472. D. I Kings 19:12-13
473. B. I Kings 19:16
474. C. I Kings 19:18
475. B. I Kings 21:9-10
476. D. II Kings 2:8
477. A. II Kings 2:9
478. C. II Kings 2:10
479. A. II Kings 2:11
480. C. II Kings 2:13-14
481. D. II Kings 2:21
482. B. II Kings 4:3-4
483. D. II Kings 4:10
484. B. II Kings 4:12
485. C. II Kings 4:41
486. C. II Kings 5:1
487. D. II Kings 5:1
488. D. II Kings 5:9
489. C. II Kings 5:10
490. A. II Kings 5:13
491. C. II Kings 5:14
492. A. II Kings 5:20
493. D. II Kings 5:27
494. A. II Kings 6:5-6
495. C. II Kings 13:21
496. A. II Kings 17:6
497. D. II Kings 18:19
498. B. II Kings 19:2
499. D. II Kings 19:35
500. B. II Kings 20:6
501. D. II Kings 20:10
502. B. II Kings 20:14-15
503. D. II Kings 22:8
504. A. II Kings 24:1
505. B. II Kings 25:26
506. C. Ezra 1:1
507. A. Ezra 3:2
508. D. Ezra 2:2
509. C. Ezra 5:1
510. C. Ezra 7:6
511. A. Ezra 9:1-2
512. C. Neh. 1:1

513. D. Neh. 1:11
514. A. Neh. 2:1
515. D. Neh. 2:5
516. C. Neh. 2:10
517. B. Neh. 6:15
518. C. Esther 1:1
519. C. Esther 1:1
520. D. Esther 1:2
521. D. Esther 1:9
522. B. Esther 1:12
523. B. Esther 2:17
524. B. Esther 2:7
525. D. Esther 2:7
526. B. Esther 2:7
527. B. Esther 2:21-22
528. A. Esther 2:22
529. A. Esther 3:1
530. D. Esther 3:2
531. B. Esther 3:9-10
532. D. Esther 4:11
533. B. Esther 4:15-16
534. D. Esther 5:4
535. B. Esther 5:7-8
536. D. Esther 5:10
537. B. Esther 5:14
538. C. Esther 6:2
539. C. Esther 6:11
540. D. Esther 7:3
541. D. Esther 7:10
542. D. Esther 8:2
543. D. Esther 9:5
544. B. Esther 9:28
545. B. Job 1:1
546. B. Job 1:6
547. B. Job 1:12
548. B. Job 1:13-19
549. D. Job 2:6
550. B. Job 2:7
551. D. Job 2:9
552. B. Job 2:11
553. C. Job 2:13
554. D. Job 38:1
555. B. Job 42:7-8
556. B. Job 42:10
557. B. Psalm headings
558. D. Ps. 23:5
559. B. Prov. 1:1
560. B. Prov. 9:10

561. A. Prov. 15:1
562. A. Prov. 31:1
563. D. Eccles. 1:2
564. B. Eccles. 3:1
565. D. Isa. 2:4
566. A. Isa. 6:1
567. C. Isa. 6:2
568. A. Isa. 7:14
569. C. Isa. 8:3
570. C. Isa. 53:4-5
571. C. Jer. 21:9
572. A. Jer. 25:11
573. C. Jer. 36:4
574. B. Jer. 37:13
575. D. Jer. 37:15
576. D. Jer. 43:6-7
577. B. Traditional author
578. C. Ezek. 1:1
579. C. Ezek. 1:3
580. D. Ezek. 2:1
581. D. Ezek. 3:2
582. B. Ezek. 37:1
583. D. Dan. 1:1
584. B. Dan. 1:7
585. D. Dan. 1:7
586. D. Dan. 2:32
587. B. Dan. 2:32
588. D. Dan. 2:32
589. B. Dan. 2:33
590. D. Dan. 2:33
591. B. Dan. 2:34
592. C. Dan. 3:1
593. C. Dan. 3:5
594. D. Dan. 3:12
595. D. Dan. 3:20
596. B. Dan. 3:22
597. B. Dan. 3:25
598. B. Dan. 3:26
599. D. Dan. 3:30
600. B. Dan. 5:5,9
601. B. Dan. 5:12
602. A. Dan. 5:30
603. A. Dan. 5:31
604. D. Dan. 6:16
605. B. Dan. 6:11-12
606. D. Dan. 6:22
607. B. Dan. 6:24
608. D. Hos. 1:2-3

609. C. Hos. 8:7
610. C. Amos 1:1
611. D. Amos 8:11
612. D. Obad. 1:1
613. D. Jonah 1:1
614. B. Jonah 1:2
615. B. Jonah 1:3
616. B. Jonah 1:3
617. D. Jonah 1:7
618. A. Jonah 1:15
619. A. Jonah 1:17
620. B. Jonah 1:17
621. B. Jonah 2:10
622. D. Jonah 3:4
623. B. Jonah 3:5
624. D. Jonah 3:10
625. B. Jonah 4:11
626. C. Mic. 5:2
627. C. Nah. 1:1
628. D. Hab. 1:6
629. D. Hag. 1:2
630. B. Mal. 3:8
631. D. Luke 1:5
632. B. Luke 1-13
633. B. Luke 1:19
634. A. Luke 1:20
635. A. Luke 1:60
636. B. Luke 2:16
637. B. Luke 2:4-5
638. D. Luke 1:26-27
639. B. Luke 1:36
640. D. Matt. 1:18-19
641. B. Matt. 1:20
642. B. Matt. 1:23
643. B. Luke 2:4
644. B. Luke 2:1
645. B. Luke 2:2
646. B. Luke 2:4
647. D. Luke 2:4
648. A. Matt. 2:1
649. A. Luke 2:4
650. D. Matt. 2:1
651. B. Luke 2:7
652. A. Luke 2:10
653. A. Luke 2:13-14
654. D. Luke 2:15
655. B. Luke 2:21
656. B. Matt. 2:1

657. C. Matt. 2:11. Three
     gifts may imply 3
     wise men.
658. A. Matt. 2:2
659. D. Mic. 5:2
660. A. Matt. 2:8
661. C. Matt. 2:11
662. D. Matt. 2:12
663. C. Matt. 2:13
664. D. Matt. 2:16
665. C. Matt. 2:19
666. D. Matt. 2:22
667. C. Matt. 2:23
668. B. Luke 2:25-26
669. B. Luke 2:36
670. B. Luke 2:39
671. D. Luke 2:41-42
672. B. Luke 2:46
673. B. Luke 2:48-49
674. A. Luke 3:2-4
675. C. Matt. 3:7
676. A. Matt. 3:11
677. D. Matt. 3:13
678. A. Matt. 3:16
679. D. Matt. 4:2
680. C. Matt. 4:3
681. C. Matt. 4:5-6
682. C. Matt. 4:8-9
683. D. Matt. 4:4,7,10
684. A. Luke 3:23
685. A. John 1:29
686. A. John 1:40
687. A. John 1:41
688. A. John 1:42
689. A. John 1:45
690. A. John 2:11
691. A. John 2:9
692. A. John 3:1-2
693. A. John 3:14
694. A. John 4:5
695. A. John 4:18
696. D. Luke 5:3
697. B. Luke 5:3,8
698. D. John 1:40
699. B. Matt. 4:18
700. D. Matt. 4:19
701. B. Matt. 4:21
702. C. Matt. 4:21

703. B. Matt. 9:9 & Mk. 2:14
704. C. Mark 2:14
705. A. Mark 3:17
706. A. Mark 3:17
707. A. John 11:16
708. B. Luke 5:29
709. B. Luke 5:27
710. A. Mark 3:14
711. B. Matt. 8:14-15
712. A. John 5:2
713. A. John 5:5
714. B. Mark 3:1-2
715. B. Matt. 12:24
716. B. Matt. 12:39
717. C. Matt. 5:3
718. D. Matt. 5:4
719. D. Matt. 5:5
720. D. Matt. 5:6
721. B. Matt. 5:7
722. D. Matt. 5:8
723. B. Matt. 5:9
724. D. Matt. 5:10
725. B. Matt. 5:11-12
726. C. Matt. 5:14
727. C. Matt. 5:44
728. D. Matt. 6:26
729. D. Matt. 6:28-29
730. B. Matt. 6:33
731. B. Matt. 7:24
732. B. Matt. 7:26
733. B. Matt. 8:8
734. C. Luke 7:11-15
735. C. Matt. 11:2-3
736. B. Matt. 14:3-4
737. C. Matt. 14:3
738. B. Matt. 14:6
739. D. Matt. 14:6-10
740. D. Matt. 18:21-22
741. D. Matt. 12:45
742. D. Luke 11-30
743. C. Luke 11:33
744. C. Luke 12:6
745. B. Luke 12:16-18
746. B. Luke 13:31-32
747. D. Luke 13:34
748. A. Matt. 13:55
749. A. Mark 5:9-12
750. B. Mark 5:12

751. B. Mark 5:13
752. C. Luke 8:41-42
753. B. Luke 8:51
754. A. Mark 5:42
755. A. Mark 5:25
756. A. John 6:1
757. A. John 6:5
758. A. John 6:8-9
759. B. John 6:9
760. B. John 6:10
761. A. John 6:13
762. A. John 6:19
763. D. Matt. 14:29
764. B. Matt. 15:38
765. B. Matt. 15:37
766. D. John 9:1-3
767. A. John 9:7
768. B. Matt. 16:13
769. B. Matt. 16:16
770. B. Matt. 17:1
771. B. Matt. 17:3
772. A. Matt. 17:4
773. A. Matt. 17:5
774. D. Matt. 17:27
775. B. Matt. 18:3
776. D. Luke 9:54
777. B. Luke 10:1
778. B. Luke 10:29-37
779. A. Luke 10:30
780. C. Luke 10:31
781. D. Luke 10:32
782. A. Luke 10:33
783. B. Luke 10:38-39
784. D. Luke 10:40
785. D. Luke 11:1
786. D. Luke 11:11
787. B. Luke 15:4
788. B. Luke 15:8
789. A. Luke 15:12
790. A. Luke 15:15
791. D. Luke 15:23
792. B. Luke 15:25-28
793. B. Luke 16:19-20
794. B. Luke 16:22
795. B. Luke 16:22-23
796. D. Luke 16:24
797. B. Luke 16:28
798. B. Luke 17:12

799. A. Luke 17:15
800. D. Luke 17:16
801. B. Luke 17:32
802. A. John 11:1
803. A. John 11:1
804. A. John 11:39
805. A. Mark 10:13
806. B. Luke 18:16
807. A. Luke 18:18,23
808. D. Mark 10:25
809. B. Mark 10:46
810. C. Luke 19:1-2
811. A. Luke 19:2
812. A. Luke 19:3-4
813. A. Luke 19:4
814. B. Luke 19:5
815. C. Luke 19:8
816. A. John 12:3
817. A. John 12:4
818. A. Matt. 21:1-2
819. D. Zech. 9:9
820. A. John 12:13
821. A. Luke 19:40
822. D. Mark 11:15
823. C. Matt. 21:13
824. C. Mark 11:13-14
825. B. Matt. 22:21
826. D. Mark 12:30
827. B. Mark 12:31
828. B. Matt. 24:37
829. C. Luke 21:24
830. B. Luke 21:33
831. C. Acts 23:8
832. A. Luke 21:2
833. B. Mark 14:3
834. D. Mark 14:5
835. D. Matt. 20:20-21
836. A. Luke 22:8
837. B. Luke 22:10
838. B. Luke 22:12
839. A. John 13:8
840. A. Luke 22:31
841. C. Luke 22:38
842. D. Matt. 26:36
843. A. Matt. 26:37
844. D. Matt. 26:40,43,45
845. B. Matt. 26:47-49
846. A. Matt. 26:15

847. B. Matt. 26:48
848. A. John 18:10
849. A. John 18:10
850. D. John 18:13
851. A. John 18:13
852. B. Matt. 27:5
853. B. Matt. 27:7
854. B. Matt. 27:2
855. A. Luke 23:7
856. D. Luke 23:6-7
857. B. Luke 23:9
858. A. John 18:38
859. D. Matt. 27:26
860. B. Matt. 27:19
861. A. John 19:12
862. B. John 19:2
863. A. Matt. 27:32
864. B. Mark 15:21
865. D. Luke 23:27-28
866. B. Luke 23:33
867. A. John 19:17
868. D. Mark 15:22
869. A. Mark 15:27
870. D. John 19:23-24
871. B. Mark 15:26
872. B. Luke 23:38
873. C. Luke 23:39-43
874. C. Matt. 27:51
875. C. Mark 15:39
876. A. John 19:32
877. A. John 19:34
878. D. John 19:38
879. D. Mark 15:44
880. A. John 19:39
881. B. Matt. 28:1
882. D. Matt. 28:5
883. B. Mark 16:9
884. B. Mark 16:9
885. A. John 20:2-4
886. A. Matt. 28:11-15
887. C. Luke 24:13
888. B. Luke 24:35
889. B. Luke 24:33
890. A. John 20:24-25
891. A. John 21:15
892. C. Acts 1:1
893. A. Acts 1:3
894. B. Acts 1:4

895. D. Acts 1:9-12
896. C. Acts 1:15
897. A. Acts 1-26
898. C. Acts 2:1
899. A. Acts 2:6
900. D. Acts 2:13
901. C. Acts 2:14
902. A. Acts 2:16
903. B. Acts 2:17
904. D. Acts 2:41
905. A. Acts 3:1
906. C. Acts 3:2
907. A. Acts 4:22
908. B. Acts 4:8
909. A. Acts 4:36
910. D. Acts 5:1-10
911. B. Acts 5:34
912. A. Acts 6:3
913. C. Acts 7:59
914. A. Acts 9:1
915. C. Acts 8:5
916. D. Acts 8:14
917. A. Acts 8:26
918. B. Acts 8:27
919. B. Acts 8:27
920. A. Acts 8:28
921. D. Acts 9:1-3
922. A. Acts 9:9
923. C. Acts 9:11
924. B. Acts 9:11
925. D. Acts 9:17-18
926. A. Acts 9:25
927. A. Acts 9:27
928. B. Acts 9:33
929. A. Acts 9:33
930. D. Acts 9:36-37
931. C. Acts 9:36
932. A. Acts 9:40
933. D. Acts 9:43
934. B. Acts 10:1
935. D. Acts 10:9-12
936. A. Acts 11:26
937. B. Acts 12:1-2
938. C. Acts 12:3
939. A. Acts 12:7
940. D. Acts 12:12
941. C. Acts 12:12
942. C. Acts 12:13-14

943. D. Acts 12:21-23
944. B. Acts 13:7
945. B. Acts 13:9
946. B. Acts 13:13
947. A. Acts 14:12
948. A. Acts 14:12
949. D. Acts 14:19
950. C. Acts 15:37-39
951. A. Acts 15:39
952. C. Acts 15:40
953. D. Acts 16:1
954. A. Acts 16:6
955. D. Acts 16:8-9
956. B. Acts 16:9
957. A. Acts 16:14
958. A. Acts 16:24-25
959. C. Acts 16:27-31
960. C. Acts 17:1,6
961. B. Acts 17:10-11
962. D. Acts 17:15
963. B. Acts 17:22
964. B. Acts 18:2
965. A. Acts 18:3
966. D. Acts 19:19
967. C. Acts 19:24
969. A. Acts 19:24
969. A. Acts 20:9
970. B. Acts 20:17
971. D. Acts 21:8
972. C. Acts 6:3-5 &
     Acts 21:8
973. B. Acts 21:9
974. A. Acts 21:27-28
975. D. Acts 21:38
976. A. Acts 22:3
977. B. Phil. 3:5
978. D. Acts 22:3
979. C. Acts 22:21-22
980. A. Acts 22:25-27
981. D. Acts 23:12-13
982. C. Acts 23:16
983. B. Acts 23:33
984. A. Acts 23:24
985. D. Acts 24:24
986. C. Acts 24:27
987. A. Acts 25:11
988. C. Acts 25:13
989. A. Acts 25:13

990. D. Acts 26:28
991. B. Acts 27:14
992. A. Acts 28:1
993. D. Acts 28:3-6
994. A. Acts 28:16
995. C. II Tim. 1:5
996. C. II Tim. 1:5
997. C. Jude 1:9
998. B. Rev. 1:4
999. B. Rev. 1:4
1000. A. Rev. 1:9
1001. D. Rev. 16:16